Teaching Guide for
Beyond the Written Word

Teaching Guide for

Beyond the Written Word
Exploring Faith Through Christian Art

Eileen M. Daily, PhD

Saint Mary's Press™

Genuine recycled paper with 10% post-consumer waste.
Printed with soy-based ink. 5094500

The publishing team included Christine Schmertz Navarro, development editor; Lorraine Kilmartin, reviewer; Mary Koehler, permissions editor; Penelope Bonnar, copy editor; James H. Gurley, typesetter; Andy Palmer, designer; manufacturing coordinated by the production services department of Saint Mary's Press.

Consultants for this book were Sheila Connolly, religion teacher at Bishop Blanchet High School, Seattle, and Laurie Dahl-Isaacson, art teacher at Bellarmine Preparatory School, Tacoma, Washington.

Printed in the United States of America

Printing: 9 8 7 6 5 4 3 2 1

Year: 2013 12 11 10 09 08 07 06 05

ISBN 0-88489-850-4

Contents

Exploring Faith Through Christian Art

Only in the past few hundred years has reading been the primary way of teaching religion. For centuries, religious education relied on hearing and seeing. Religious education can benefit from a return to the ages-old methods of hearing and seeing to complement reading. *Beyond the Written Word: Exploring Faith Through Christian Art* and this teaching guide enable you to make one of the old ways—seeing—available to twenty-first-century students. This introduction offers a brief history of Christian art, an explanation of the value of art in religious education today, a survey of this book, and some hints for starting out.

How the Old Ways Grew the Faith

In the earliest days of Christian art, the stonemasons and jewelers who made art for people of all faiths and cultures also made sarcophagi and signet rings for Christians. By the end of the fourth century, monks were making Christian images, better known as icons. Monks also illuminated the bibles and prayer books of the Middle Ages. In western Europe, religious people conceived the decorative parts of the design and architecture of the great Romanesque and Gothic cathedrals, and members of the artisan guilds executed their ideas.

Artists, as we understand that word today, first emerged as the Middle Ages ended and the Renaissance began. By the end of the fifteenth century, artists were the heroes and stars of the day. Some artists—Michelangelo, for one—were committed to their faith, theological study, and living a good life. Other artists lived less-faithful lives but were renowned for the religious paintings they made for the Church.

As Europeans conquered other parts of the world, they brought the Catholic faith with them, often in the form of art. The missionaries thought art would circumvent the language barriers and help communicate the faith to the people of the Americas, Asia, and Africa. Artists all over the globe in turn learned to blend the content and styles of the Christian art from Europe with their own styles and media. Today, Christian artists are working all over the world. The student book contains art from various cultures.

Why Use Art in Religious Education Today?

High school religious educators seek additional ways to work with religious art in their classrooms. Using religious art in teaching is not only effective but also a great way to include learning skills other than those used in reading, lecture, and discussion. Two challenges, however, can deter teachers from regularly using art. First, finding enough good reproductions of a painting to distribute to each student in a class is difficult. Second, many religion teachers feel that teaching art is beyond their expertise.

Beyond the Written Word's student resource and this teacher's guide solve both those problems. Because the student resource contains the images, you will not have to find ways to make the art visible to everyone in the class. In addition, the teaching guide leads you through the process of using art in class with the students.

Educational and psychological theories support the use of art in education. Church history and solid theology support the incorporation of art into religious education. This manual does not have enough space to expound on this theory. The manual does offer an introduction to teaching with art in the religion classroom so that you can increase your visual literacy and comfort level with reading and interpreting art in the context of the school's religious education curriculum.

To increase visual literacy, I recommend basic books such as *Art for Beginners,* by Dani Cavallaro, and *A Primer of Visual Literacy,* by Donis A. Dondis, for learning the language of art. Appendix 2 lists publication information for these and other resources. Ask a colleague who teaches art to recommend a basic art history book you can use as a general reference.

How to Use *Beyond the Written Word*

The Student Book

The student book contains reproductions of twenty-two works of art from many corners of the Christian world. The artworks are large enough for students to see the details of the images. Each piece of art is used in at least one activity in the teaching guide. Much of the art is used in several activities because most paintings can be viewed from several perspectives. For example, a painting of the Wise Men's visit to the infant Jesus can be viewed for what it says about Jesus, for what it says about Mary and Joseph, and for what it says about the Wise Men.

The Teaching Guide

This teacher's resource guides and supports you as you teach concepts using the art in the student book. In addition, it will show you how to continue to use art in religious education with art that is not in the student book.

- **Chapter 1.** This first chapter has five models for using art in the classroom. These models help you determine what questions to ask and which processes to use with students, depending on the way you want to approach a piece of art. Read through these models carefully. Not only will you learn skills for using these activities, but you will also recognize some of the same approaches throughout the teaching guide. The models will also help you create your own activities, using art and subject matter you choose.
- **Chapters 2 through 5.** These four chapters roughly follow the structure of the *Catechism of the Catholic Church.* Each chapter offers activities about specific concepts based on the artwork in the student component of *Beyond the Written Word.*
- **Appendix 1: More About the Art.** This appendix provides background for the twenty-two pieces of art in the student book. The background pieces present information to help analyze an artwork for its theological, moral, and social relevance, and in a style young people might connect with. This breadth should spark creativity and curiosity in you and the students so that they will want to research the artworks or the artists more fully.

  The background information does not have to be shared with the students for many of the exercises. The material is in the appendix so you can prepare by familiarizing yourself with the art, and pursue suggested leads for finding more information if the students are interested in knowing more. In a few activities, the preparation step alerts you to the importance of reading the background information in order to prepare for the class.
- **Appendix 2: Additional Resources.** This appendix provides a bibliography and suggestions for more resources for your classroom or for your own enrichment.

How Does This Book Fit into Your Curriculum?

Although the activities in this teaching guide relate to the catechetical material you present to your students, the book is not catechetical. Instead, it is a resource that offers supplementary activities to enhance the students' learning of the concepts you are teaching them as part of the regular curriculum. The activities in this manual will make sense to the students only if they have a good grasp of the concepts referenced in the activities. In most cases, you will need to present the concept before supplementing your presentation with the art.

Because this resource might also be used in an art class, each activity provides references to relevant material in *The Catholic Faith Handbook for Youth (CFH).* Published by Saint Mary's Press, the *CFH* presents catechism material in a teen-friendly way. Should you want to look up some background material for an activity, the *CFH* is a good place to start.

Getting Started

The first step toward using these resources is to read the introduction in the student book. It offers a quick example of the way art can augment religious education lessons. If you are protesting that "I don't know anything about art," be assured that you do not need to know anything about art to make this process work. By disclosing your ignorance of art to the students, you make the activities a joint exploration of the artwork rather than a question-and-answer exercise. Images that provide only answers are not art. Good art always asks us questions.

The second step is to experiment with a few of the activities in chapters 2 through 5. These activities are geared toward concepts that are part of a standard religion curriculum and offer step-by-step instructions. A number of these activities are structured so they can be easily adapted for additional lessons with other works of art.

Finally, chapter 1, "Models for Teaching with Art," offers five templates that contain everything you need to let your creative side loose. If you were to analyze the activities in chapters 2 through 5, you would find that most of them are variations on these general approaches.

Words of Encouragement

Enjoy and trust this process that has been done with depth and insight by millions of Christians—who may or may not have been able to read and write—throughout Christian history.

You know the elements of the faith, you know the moral teachings of the Church, you know the Bible. You just have to learn to read them in the language of art.

You are invited to discover the life Christians through the ages have found in art.

Chapter 1

Models for Teaching with Art

Overview

This chapter offers you material at three levels. First are the basic activity models that give you skills for teaching the other activities in the book. Second, these are real activities that offer concrete ways of using art in the classroom. Last, the activities are templates that help you shape and create your own activities. All but the fourth model activity can be done with either the paintings in the student book or with images you or the students gather.

Activities

- Reading a Painting
- Archaeology and Art
- Art and Spiritual Growth
- Breaking Open the Scriptures with Art
- Becoming the Religious Artist

Reading a Painting

In this activity, students use art to recognize the depth and the many facets of any particular Christian concept or Scripture story.

Preparation
- Choose a painting from *Beyond the Written Word* or from another source according to the recommendations under "Art."
- To prepare for step 3 of the activity, look up symbols depicted in the painting in a dictionary of Christian symbolism (see app. 2), or make the dictionary available to the students and have them research the symbols.
- Go through the following exercise yourself first.

How to Read a Painting

When the students struggle to engage with a painting, offer the following suggestions and questions:

- Compare the biblical story to the painting, if relevant. What is missing? What has been added?

- Notice facial expressions and what they reveal about the emotions of the people in the painting.

- Notice hands, both what they are doing and how they are depicted.

- Notice postures, gestures, stances, and attitudes reflected in body positioning.

Offer the following additional questions and suggestions and have the students consider their answers with the painting's story in mind:

- Notice the overall mood. For example, how does the mood affect the story being told?

- Notice the use of light and shadow in the painting and how it creates emphasis or drama.

- Notice the use of color in the painting and how it creates harmony or tension between the elements of the paintings.

- Notice the lines of the painting. Are they actual lines or are the figures and objects forming lines? (Actual lines might form the cross while the shape of Christ's body on it might create another crosslike shape.) The lines in garments, in landscapes, in architecture might all come into play, or a painting might not have any evident lines. Are the lines curved or straight? Are they vertical, horizontal, or diagonal? Do they direct the attention toward anything in particular?

- Notice the shapes and the forms in the painting. For example, do any lines form a triangle that might indicate the Trinity? Are the shapes angular or rounded?

- Notice the way time is depicted in the painting. For example, is it a snapshot of a single moment or are many moments depicted at once? Does the scene illustrate busy people or figures moving at a slower pace?

- Notice the texture of the painting. Is it smooth and refined, is it rough and earthy, or is it more subtle than either extreme?

- Notice the objects depicted in the painting, both the ones that seem central and the ones that seem peripheral, or hidden.

Art

You will want to select art that reflects the concept the students are studying. One approach is to think of a Scripture story that reflects the concept, then find paintings of that story. When you first do exercises like this, you might want to use images that are rich in religious symbolism. European images from AD 1350 to AD 1650 would be good choices.

1. Give each student a copy of the image, or project the image onto a screen using either a computer or a slide projector. Invite the students to examine the art for a few minutes in silence. Ask the students to call out things they noticed about the image from their examination of it. Record their observations on the board. (Have a lot of board space available because the list is likely to be long.)

2. When the students have run out of observations, draw their attention to specific details in the painting. Use the questions in "How to Read a Painting," on page 11 of this teaching guide, to help the students recognize more elements. Record their additional observations in a new column. The combined lists of details should be substantial. If necessary, try to generate more details by asking the students to consider additional design elements, such as the pairs of qualities found in "How to Help Students Clarify Their Responses to Art," on page 18 of this guide. Record these new observations in a new column. When you are satisfied that the combined lists contain enough details, ask the students to observe the differences between the list of their initial observations and the subsequent lists of details generated after you asked more questions. This part of the activity helps the students sharpen their observation skills.

3. The next step is to discern whether the painting contains any symbolism that might not be obvious to the average adolescent. Share with the students your list of the symbols and their meanings that you found in the painting during your preparation for this activity. Add your list to the lists on the board. If you did not prepare a list of symbols beforehand, ask the students to research the symbolic meanings of people, objects, colors, and gestures that have particular significance in the Christian context. Have a dictionary of Christian symbols available for the students to facilitate their research.

You might need to guide the students through their research by offering examples of Christian symbols commonly found in art. For example, a palm branch carried in someone's hand or arm often indicates that the person is a martyr. Add any symbolism they find to the list on the board.

4. Invite the students (in small or large groups) to determine what the painting has to say about the concept they are studying. Suggest that they refer to both the painting and the list of observations on the board. When an interpretation of the concept fails to account for one or more of the observations made, draw the students' attention to that detail and explore it in greater depth.

Archaeology and Art

In this activity, students use a painting to learn more about the Christian community of a particular time and place.

This activity is ideal for a Church history course but could also be used in any course about the culture of another time. It also works as part of an interdisciplinary project between the religion and social studies departments. An activity such as this could be used to compare the religious priorities of Catholics with those of Lutherans in the sixteenth century.

Preparation

- Select one piece of art, or several from the same time period and place. For example, you might choose four or five paintings from mid-fourteenth-century Siena, Italy.
- Do some initial research about the painter, or painters, and the time period:
    - **Artists.** If possible, research the artists' lives and circumstances for information about any of the artists' patrons and their agendas. If you cannot gather specific information, the paintings will provide enough information for speculation. You need only have the time period and the place involved.

    - **Time period.** Familiarize yourself with the general details of the relevant history of the time: the conflicts, the politics, the economics, the social and cultural situation, the Church, the faith of the people, and so on. Find as much information as you can in a thirty-minute Web or library search.

Choose questions for step 4 from "How to Dig into a Painting," on page 15 of this teaching guide, that seem appropriate for the selected.

Art

Select at least four pieces of Christian art from any time and any place. Although Renaissance Europe is often the first source that comes to mind, other cultures that have been exposed to the Good News have created art. Finding pre-twentieth-century Asian and African Christian art is difficult, but some Ethiopian Orthodox art is available from as far back as the fifth century. Latin American and North American Christian art can be found at museum Web sites and in books. (See app. 2 for resource ideas.) Especially when you first start using this method, choose paintings that have a recognizable time period.

1. Provide each student with a copy of each image, or project the images on a screen. If necessary, create a slide show of the images. Begin by inviting the students to look at the art for a few minutes.

Tell the students they are going to use these paintings as archaeological evidence to uncover the culture as well as the cultural and religious beliefs and practices of the people of the century the art was created. Set the scene for them by making the following points:
- The community where an artist lives and worships influences that artist. The artist is also affected by family, upbringing, and social, political, and economic factors. If an artist created a painting at the request of a patron, that piece of art will likely reflect something about the patron.

○ When an artist makes a painting, she or he includes some details intentionally and others just because they are the way things are done at that time in that place. For example, the artist may be careful about how the people are painted but may use the same bright, muted, or earthy color palate all artists of that time and place used. Therefore, all elements of a piece of art tell us something even if the artist did not intend them to.

○ An archaeologist who pulls a ring out of a dig site compares the ring's markings, the material it is made from, the size, the workmanship, and so on, with what is already known about jewelry of that time. The ring then either adds to or challenges what the archaeologist already knows about the civilization being uncovered. We are going to do the same with paintings.

○ Getting to know the people or the circumstances of another society is a lot like getting to know someone you've just met and involves asking many questions. We start with questions that are based on what we see. Dark paintings might inspire us to ask, was this a depressed community? A painting of a small room might prompt us to inquire about the living conditions of the time, and so on.

2. Invite the students to pose questions about the paintings you have presented. Write their questions on the board.

3. Ask the students what they already know about life and religious beliefs in the region and from the time period of the paintings. Invite them to contribute answers to the questions raised in step 2. For the questions they cannot answer, offer answers based on your research of the artists, the time period, and the place. Your answers should provide a background for the students but not give them more information than they requested. Do not feel obligated to have more answers than you do. Conclude by saying:
○ We have begun to make the acquaintance of this community, but we will have to dig deeper to get to know it better.

4. Continue to guide the students' investigation of the paintings by asking questions you selected from "How to Dig into a Painting" during your preparation. Record their answers on the board.

5. Point out to the students that they have been successful in collecting data about the society they are studying. Tell them it is now time to become cultural anthropologists who will construct a description of the culture, beliefs, and practices of the people that created the artifacts. Have the students form small groups. Tell them that each group is to use the information on the board to write a description of the community. If there is a specific religious belief, practice, or cultural trait you wish to emphasize, ask the students to focus their description in that direction. Explain to the students that any feature common to all the paintings probably is a reflection of the community but that a feature found in only one painting might not be. Allow a few minutes for the students to write the descriptions.

How to Dig into a Painting

Basic Questions

- Who is represented? Who is left out?
- What topic did the artist consider important enough to make a painting of it?
- When was the artwork made? Does it represent the artist's era or another time? Or is it a combination of the two? Does it depict real time or sacred time (the time of eternity or heaven or prayer)? Or is it a combination of the two?
- Where is the action taking place? Is it inside or outside? Is it in some faraway place or where the painting was made?
- Why was it painted? Why was this topic chosen?

Religious Questions

- What was this community's relationship with God?
- What was this community afraid of?
- Did this community experience a lot of suffering? How did it understand suffering?
- Did this community experience a lot of evil? How did it understand evil?
- What gave this community joy?
- How did this community express love?
- How did this community understand salvation?
- What was the relationship between this community and Creation?

Political Questions

- Who was in power at the time and who was not?
- How was political power exercised (money and influence, arms and fighting, and so on)?
- How did the people without power feel about those who had it?
- How did the people with power feel about those without? (Or did they even think about them?)
- How much freedom to speak their minds did average people have?
- Who had basic political rights and who did not?
- Did the Church have political power? In whose favor did it exercise that power?

Economic Questions

- How were artists paid? Who paid them?
- Who had money and who did not?
- What economic opportunities were available to which people?
- What was the economic and political agenda of the person or institution that paid the artist?
- What economic structure does the painting try to communicate to the viewer?
- Did the Church have economic power? In whose favor did it exercise that power?

Social Questions

- How were ethnic minorities viewed and treated?
- How were people of other religions viewed and treated?
- How were children viewed and treated?
- How were women viewed and treated?
- How much did the Church influence social relationships within the family, village, city, and so on?
- Were people formal and polite or casual and coarse?
- Did groups exhibit different social norms? How was the society split?

6. Have the students present their religious and cultural descriptions, and then share any additional information you have about the culture that affirms or challenges their descriptions. Be sure the discussion includes student findings related to the religious themes relevant to the course.

7. As you conclude the activity, suggest to the students that every culture, including their own, discloses its religious, political, economic, and social beliefs and structures in the images it produces.

Try This

To further hone the archaeological skills of the students and to offer an opportunity to reflect on the modern culture, do this activity with several pieces of modern art, magazine covers, or other images that reveal something about our society today.

Art and Spiritual Growth

In this activity, students recognize the link between their emotional responses to images and their spiritual growth.

Preparation

Gather a variety of religious art images, enough so that each student will have one, from *Beyond the Written Word* or from another collection of images as suggested in the next section, "Art."

Art

A number of approaches to the selection process can be taken, including the following methods:

• To introduce the students to art and religion, choose a random collection of Christian art.
• To help the students identify what matters most to them about a given subject, select images of that subject from a variety of styles—for example, the Crucifixion.
• To help the students reflect on their personal relationship with Jesus, find images that portray Jesus at different ages.
• To focus the students on a particular aspect of the Christian faith, limit your selection to one artistic time period—for example, Baroque religious art. Such a limit helps learners focus on those aspects of the faith that attract them regardless of the artistic style.

1. Invite the students to look through the artworks, with each selecting the image they find most appealing or interesting. Have the students gaze at their chosen images for a few moments. Next, ask the students to each take a turn naming the one thing they like most about their image. The first time you do this activity, you may hear "I don't know, I just like it." If that happens, use the techniques in "How to Help Students Clarify Their Responses to Art," on page 18 of this guide, to help the students unpack their feelings about the painting.

2. When the students have identified what they like about the painting, ask them to each summarize their responses to the class in one to two sentences. Then offer them the following thoughts for their reflection:

How to Help Students Clarify Their Responses to Art

At times, teens will respond to art neutrally or strongly, yet have a hard time articulating why. Use these tips to help your students understand their reactions:

- Have the students cover different halves of the painting in turn (top, bottom, left, right) and look at the painting. Ask them this question:
  - Do you still have the same response to the painting with each view?

- Ask the students to consider the answers to these questions:
  - If the people, or other major features, were not in the painting, would you have the same response to it?

  - What if just some of the people were not in the painting?

  - Which people or features are essential to the feeling of the painting?

- Invite the students to imagine the same painting reproduced on a black-and-white copier. Ask them these questions:
  - Would you still be drawn to it?

  - What if the brightness were turned down and the same colors were present but muted?

  - Would it still grab you?

- Read the following introductory phrase and pairs of words. Ask the students to jot down which word of each pair inspires strong feelings in them one way or another.
  - This painting is . . .

  - spacious or cozy

  - orderly or zany

  - simple or complex

  - subtle or bold

  - concrete or fuzzy

  - understated or exaggerated

  - active or still

  - busy or quiet

- Ask the students this question:
  - If the same story were painted with a different mood, would you like it as much?

○ You have identified and summarized the qualities of your painting that you find attractive. Where do you encounter, experience, or receive these same qualities today? What could you do to encounter, experience, or receive more of these qualities? For example, if you are attracted to the warmth of a painting, how might you encounter, experience, or receive more warmth in your life?

3. Invite the students to again examine their images. Ask them to consider whether their artworks depict a person, action, mood, stance, attitude, or way of being someone or something they would like to imitate. If the students are comfortable with one another, invite them to work in pairs or triads. In their groups, have each student name what he or she would like to imitate. Then have the other members of their group offer suggestions on how to carry out that imitation. For example, how might a student who is drawn to the bravery of a character in a painting increase his or her own bravery?

If the students do not form groups, invite them each to brainstorm in writing how they might be able to imitate the person, action, mood, stance, attitude, or way of being they named.

4. Finally, ask the students to examine their lives to see whether they are doing anything that keeps them from adopting the qualities they named in step 2 or from imitating the person, action, mood, stance, attitude, or way of being they named in step 3. Invite them to reflect on ways they can reduce the behavior they have identified. Offer the following sample questions, which the students might ask themselves:

○ What keeps me from warmth or from warm people?

○ What keeps me from being brave?

Offer the following comments to the students:

○ When we identify the qualities that attract us or the ways of being that we would like to imitate, we get in touch with desires for goodness that God has placed deep within us. These desires are gifts from God. Viewing religious art can be like reading a biblical passage where our own responses can tell us about the spiritual longings that dwell within us.

Identifying spiritual longings and the roadblocks to attaining them can illuminate obstacles to our spiritual growth. We can then ask God for the grace to overcome the obstacles or to strategize with others about ways we can encounter the gifts that God wants to give us.

5. Close by encouraging the students to become more aware of the images in their world that attract them and what the makers of those images want them to imitate.

Activity Extension

Saint Ignatius learned discernment initially by comparing his internal responses to knightly tales of heroism with his responses to the lives of the saints. After reading one type of book and then the other, he noticed a difference in the responses they evoked. Although both types of books inspired a positive response in him, the lives of the saints evoked a spirit that was long-lasting. The tales about heroes, however, initially excited him, but then the enthusiasm dissipated.

In a similar reflection process, guide the students through this activity using both religious art and modern print advertising images that target teens. Ask the students to note what attracts them to the advertising and to then determine what details draw them to the religious art.

Breaking Open the Scriptures with Art

This activity helps the students gain an appreciation of biblical interpretation, or *hermeneutics*, and become conscious of the preconceptions they bring to their interpretations of the Scriptures.

Preparation

- Choose a well-known Scripture passage, and gather a collection of images that illustrustrate it.
- Read or review the passage, and then examine each image, noting the differences and the similarities in how the paintings tell the story.
- Have a Bible on hand.

Art

Images of specific Scripture stories are available from a variety of resources. (See app. 2 for specifics about these resources.)

1. Choose a student who is an expressive reader to read the relevant passage from the Bible aloud, or read it aloud yourself. Ask the students to listen carefully as the passage from the Bible is read, allowing the story to unfold like a movie in their minds.

2. Invite the students to identify the most significant elements of the story. Record on the board the common themes indicated in the students' responses.

3. Explain to the students how they can compare art with the biblical stories the art illustrates. Tell them that artists fill in details that the Bible stories do not include. Offer the students the following example:

- The Bible tells us that Adam and Eve ate the fruit of the tree of knowledge of good and evil. A painter must make that fruit look like a fruit. Which fruit does the painter choose?

Show the students the first image you chose for this activity, and ask them to identify those details that the artist thought were significant. When they identify an element that corresponds to a theme from the list you recorded in step 2, place a tick or check mark next to it. For elements that don't fit any of the themes, add an appropriate theme to the list.

Now ask the students to identify the elements the artist included in the image that they did not visualize when the story was being read.

Complete these first steps with the other paintings.

4. After you have presented each painting once, return to the first image. Ask the students whether they now notice more details in the image. Record any additional details they identify. Then draw the students' attention to the differences among the images that you noticed during your preparation that the students have not identified. Be willing to jump around from image to image as the discussion unfolds. Use the questions in "How to

How to Compare Images of the Same Biblical Story

Ask the students the following sets of questions to help them distinguish the differences between the images of the same biblical story, including their own visualization of the story:

- o Does the character exhibit different emotions in some of the paintings, and are different emotions possible given the details of the story? Do any differences in emotion change how the story comes across in the painting?

- o Do all the paintings depict the action the same way? Do the various depictions of the action all seem possible given the actual words in the Bible story? Do the differences in the way the action is portrayed change how the story comes across in the painting?

- o Do all the paintings depict God (Father, Son, or Spirit) the same way? Does the Bible story tell us what God looked like in this event? What meaning can we glean from the way an artist depicts God? Are the images of God in any of the paintings similar to your mental picture of God before you looked at the images? For example, how did God look when you played the story in your mind?

- o Do all the paintings have the same number of people present at the event? What difference does it make if more or fewer people are depicted? Does the number of people present make a difference in how the story comes across in the painting?

Compare Images of the Same Biblical Story," on page 21 of this guide, to help the students compare the paintings.

5. Invite another student to reread the Bible passage, or read it yourself. Ask the students to close their eyes during the reading, listening again to the story and letting the movie roll in their minds. After the reading, ask the students to name details they noticed during this second read. Draw their attention to the list of significant elements from step 2. Ask whether they would stick with that original list or add to it. Add any other observations the students make.

6. Invite discussion about what this exercise teaches about reading and interpreting the Bible. Make the following observations and again invite the students' input:

- What people believe and know affects how they interpret a story.

- A single reading or interpretation of the Bible is less meaningful than multiple readings or interpretations of the same story.

- The interpreter (reader, artist, or viewer) automatically fills in the details the Bible leaves out, and every interpreter does that differently.

- Most of the paintings share the most important meanings of a biblical story. However, the details may differ because each artist determines the significance of the details depending on her or his circumstances, which include the artist's time and place of residence in history.

7. Invite the students to recall the lessons they learned from this activity when they read the Bible or any other text.

Becoming the Religious Artist

In this activity, the students become the artists who create religious art.

Preparation
- Consult with the art teacher about the level of skill you can expect from the students. If the art curriculum includes skills the students should already have learned, then it is fair to expect that the students will create religious artworks that live up to the art department's standards.
- List the qualities you expect in the students' finished artwork on the back of a photocopy of handout 1, "Creating a Piece of Religious Art."
- Ask the art teacher to help you assess the student artwork based on these qualities when the assignment is complete.
- Make one two-sided copy of your photocopy of handout 1 for each student.

Art
The students will select images from *Beyond the Written Word* that help them develop their own artworks.

1. Share the following thoughts with your students in your own words:
- Consider that many artists use visual images to convey qualities or truths, which are invisible or intangible.

o The very process of creating art increases an artist's spiritual insight. Artwork, then, exists to help the viewer understand those spiritual truths.

o The process of making such a work of art may increase the artist's own insight into the spiritual truth. You have the opportunity to experience this creative process firsthand.

o You will not simply be left to your own devices. The class as a whole will do three major steps in the creative process.

2. Inform the students that the first major step in creating the art is to explore the spiritual concepts or truths. Share the truths you want the students to explore, whether those truths be discipleship, faith, or the Church as one, holy, catholic, and apostolic. (See the "One, Holy, Catholic, Apostolic" activity in chapter 2.) Then lead a brainstorming exercise to create lists of synonyms and images that the students associate with these words or the concept. Fully develop these lists, exploring how the words and images relate to the main concept.

3. Explain to the students that the second step they will take is to explore how other artists have visualized the same concepts. Invite them to look through the images in *Beyond the Written Word* (or another collection you compile) to find paintings or parts of paintings that either blatantly or subtly convey the concept. Give the students 10 minutes to discuss as a class how each image they found conveys the topic they are studying. Then ask the students to select the two or three images they think best communicate the concept.

4. The third step involves asking questions. For each image selected as representative of the concept, ask the students the questions found in "How to Think Like an Artist," on page 24 of this guide.

5. Instruct the students as follows:
o Through art, you have explored the concept we have been studying. You have found images that other artists have used to represent this concept. You have analyzed those images to determine four things: (1) how well they conveyed the message, (2) how attractive they are, (3) how relevant they are, and (4) how layered they are.

Explain the assignment and distribute handout 1 to the students to use as a guide. If you are asking students to create their art in class, provide a good selection of media for them to use. Ideally, students will complete the project on their own at home over the course of a week.

6. After the students have finished their projects, share their artworks with the class. Give the students time to examine each image. If the students seem mature and respectful of one another, invite them to ask questions similar to those you asked during their exploration of the professional artists' work in steps 3 and 4 of this activity. To create an environment safe from harsh criticism, ask the students to limit their comments to the elements of the work that meet the criteria: communicates the concept, attractive, relevant, and layered in meaning.

How to Think Like an Artist

With images by other artists as a starting point, help the students translate a Christian concept into modern understanding by offering the following questions and tips:

- Are you attracted to this image, and do you think others in your time and place would find it attractive?

- How could the image be modified to make it more attractive to you or to your peers, assuming you had the skill to make the changes?

- Does the image convey its spiritual message with subtlety and layers of meaning or with simplicity and the obvious?

- If the message is subtle, determine whether it is too subtle for today's viewers. If it is too subtle, how would you change it? Assuming you had the skill, would you eliminate some layers but make sure people knew to look for the remaining layers?

- If the message is obvious, determine whether it is too obvious for today's sophisticated viewers. If it is too obvious, how would you change it? Would you add some layers and nuance but make it possible for viewers to still get the message?

- Is the image relevant enough to the present time and place (note that relevant is not the same as attractive) that the message is communicated in a way that matters to people?

- How would you modify the image to make it more relevant to the present time and place, assuming you had the skill to make the modifications?

Creating a Piece of Religious Art

Create a work of art that conveys the assigned concept in an attractive, relevant, layered, and effective way.

The Assignment

- An excellent assignment will be attractive, relevant, and layered in its meanings, and will convey the meaning of the concept. These qualities are described below. A good grade will also depend on your using the skills you have learned in art classes. (This is the same as having to use correct spelling and grammar as well as complete sentences and paragraphs when you write a paper.)
- You can use any medium, including computer graphics.
- You can build upon other artworks as you would on other people's ideas in a paper. You can do this either by copying a portion of a work or by sampling on the computer. Your work *cannot* be a miscellaneous collection of samples from other people's works. If you sample, you must provide references. (Note that the title of the Van Gogh painting on page 19 of the student book *Beyond the Written Word: Exploring Faith Through Christian Art* tells the viewer that the artist copied Delacroix's painting.) If the famous Van Gogh can do it, so can you. (If you want to see what is possible in making an old painting new, find a copy of Delacroix's original work and compare it with Van Gogh's painting.)
- Do not make a collage of magazine images.
- Have fun.

Questions to Ask Yourself as You Work

- Is this work attractive?
  - Is this work attractive to me and will it be attractive to other people in this place and time?
- Is this work relevant?
  - Is the image relevant (not the same question as attractive) enough to the present time and place so that the meaning is likely to get communicated in a way that matters to peers?
- Is this worked layered in meaning?
  - Is this work subtle (its meaning does not hit you over the head) and layered (has several levels of meaning) in a balanced way?
  - If it is subtle, will the viewers understand all the layers of meaning, or will it be too obscure or unfamiliar to them?
  - If it is obvious, is it too obvious for today's viewers? Does it require more layers and nuance?
- Does this work communicate the concept? (You may want to ask a few people about this to test out how well it communicates the concept.)

(The material in this handout is adapted from "Seeing and Being Seen: A Visual Approach to Religious Education," PhD dissertation, Boston College, 2001, by Eileen Mary Daily.)

Chapter 2

The Creed

Overview

This chapter has several activities to help the students talk about God as Father, Son, and Holy Spirit. This chapter also includes an activity that challenges students to create their own religious art about the Church.

Activities

God the Father
- "God, the Father, the Almighty"
- God, "Maker of Heaven and Earth"

God the Son
- Jesus Christ Is True God and True Man
- Recognizing Jesus After the Resurrection
- The Way to the Last Judgment

God the Holy Spirit
- "We Believe in the Holy Spirit"

The Church
- One, Holy, Catholic, Apostolic

"God, the Father, the Almighty"

The students will explore the all-powerful nature of God the Father through a painting by Michelangelo. This activity is a natural precursor to "God, 'Maker of Heaven and Earth,'" the activity that follows it.

Preparation
- Before the class, examine the details the painter attributes to God in the painting. Reflect and allow metaphorical relationships to form in your own mind before you invite the students to do so.

- Read or review Genesis 1:1-25.
- See pages 43-44 of *The Catholic Faith Handbook for Youth (CFH)* for background relevant to this activity.
- Have a Bible on hand.

Art

This activity uses the artwork *The Creation of Adam*, on page 9 in *Beyond the Written Word*.

1. Tell the students that artists often use visual objects and attributes to represent spiritual or invisible truths, the same way writers paint a mental image using similes and metaphors.

Invite the students to direct their attention to *The Creation of Adam*. Ask the students to each list the physical characteristics Michelangelo gave God. Then, invite students to share their observations. Make a composite list of their observations on the board so all the characteristics the students came up with are represented. Ask the students to hold their observations about God's clothing or other people in the painting for later. If any of the following details are missing from the list, ask the students leading questions to help them identify these details in the painting, and then add them to the list. (This approach helps them train their eyes to see more than they usually see.)
- God is suspended above the earth.
- God has muscular arms and legs.
- God has a big, muscular chest.
- God's face is focused or intent.
- God has hair, a moustache, and a beard that are gray.
- God's visible ear is big.
- God's nose is long and straight and big.
- God's body is energized from the tip of his finger to his feet.
- God seems to be moving fast, but he doesn't seem to be in a hurry to shift his attention from Adam.
- God's energy does not seem strained; he is not stretching or straining toward Adam, just reaching.

2. Invite the students to use the list on the board to identify the spiritual characteristics they think Michelangelo may have been trying to portray with each physical trait. Allow the students to make the symbolic connections without your suggesting any possibilities. Here are some examples:
- God moves through the air: God can go anywhere.
- God has a big ear and nose: God has ears to hear the faintest cry and a nose to smell the slightest wrong.
- God has gray hair: God's wisdom is infinite, but God's youthful and muscular body symbolizes infinite energy and power.
- God has a large chest: God has infinite Spirit.
- God is moving forward: God is aware of the world but at the same time focused on Adam, a solitary creature.
- God does not show strain or stress: God is infinitely energetic.

Wrap up this discussion with a focus on the word *almighty.* Do all these physical and spiritual attributes communicate that God is almighty?

3. Invite the students to return their attention to Michelangelo's painting. This time draw their attention to Adam, the woman under God's left arm, and the relationship of those two figures to God. Focus first on Adam. Ask the students to notice Adam's gaze toward God's face. Ask them to list some adjectives that describe the gaze. Then invite them to notice how the woman is using God's arm and body as she gazes at Adam. Ask the students to describe the position of God's arm in relationship to the woman. Have them consider what the woman might want from God in this moment. Have them describe what God is doing in relationship to the woman. Record their answers, including their lists of adjectives, on the board. You should get answers that include some of the following elements:

- Adam is looking at God with complete devotion, attention, submission, love, respect, and anything else seen in his gaze.
- The woman is seeking safety, protection, security, a solid shield, home, and anything else seen in her posture and face.
- God has wrapped his arm around the woman in a gesture of protection, love, presence, here and now, and anything else seen in the gesture.

Note that many people have speculated that the woman is Eve.

4. Invite the students to use the list generated in step 2 to identify the spiritual characteristics of God that Michelangelo might have been trying to portray. Those characteristics all point to God as Father who provides love, protection, presence, safety, home, and a solid shield, gifts that inspire devotion, love, submission, and respect from those whom God gifts. Wrap up this discussion with a focus on the word *Father.* Distinguish between what our human fathers are able to bring to their fatherly relationships and what the "almighty" God is able to bring to such a relationship.

Bring the activity to a close by summarizing the spiritual characteristics relating to God's being "Almighty" and "Father," which the students uncovered in the painting.

God, "Maker of Heaven and Earth"

In this activity, students look at Michelangelo's portrayal of God in terms of his role as "maker of heaven and earth, of all that is seen and unseen." This activity focuses on the same painting used in the previous activity. Because the two activities complement each other, you may want to do both of them.

Preparation
See pages 44-46 of the *CFH* for background information relevant to this activity.

Art
This activity uses the artwork *The Creation of Adam,* on page 9 in *Beyond the Written Word.*

1. Draw the students' attention to *The Creation of Adam.* Ask them to focus on God's and Adam's hands. Point out that Michelangelo places this link between them in the center of the painting. This slight touch between God and human is enough, is all God has to do, and the human being lives.

Suggest that Michelangelo has more to say about Creation in this painting. Ask the students to point out what the artist includes in the painting to emphasize God as "maker of heaven and earth." Michelangelo includes fairly obvious references to heaven and earth. Angels (heavenly creatures), who existed before Adam, are floating around God. Adam is reclining on a patch of grass on earth.

2. In your own words, share some of the following observations with the students:

- ○ Michelangelo may not have been content to include only the obvious references to the Creator. Look at the red drape behind God in relation to the rest of the painting. Soften or blur your gaze while looking at the silhouette of the grouping that includes the red drape, God, the angels, and the other drapes. Does this resemble something you have seen before? (Invite their ideas.)

- ○ The scientist Frank Meshberger has suggested that Michelangelo may have intended this grouping to look like a side-view cross section of the human brain. Of course, we will never know what Michelangelo intended, but we know he was familiar with what the brain looked like. If Michelangelo intended to put that physical symbol in the painting, what spiritual meaning was he trying to convey?

- ○ The Nicene Creed notes that God created "all that is seen and unseen." An image resembling the human brain might represent the unseen of God's Creation that human beings do not understand. (Invite comments on the unseen element.)

3. Ask the students whether they think that Michelangelo expected the everyday viewers of his paintings to get this much spiritual meaning out of the painting. If some students answer no, ask them whether they would change their minds if they knew that the Sistine Chapel was used only for popes, cardinals, and bishops for many years. Ask them whether they think that most tourists who pass through the chapel today grasp the spiritual meaning of the painting. If any of the students have gone to the Sistine Chapel, ask them to talk about their visits.

Jesus Christ Is True God and True Man

In this activity, the students will explore the mystery of Jesus Christ's identity as true God and true Man through artists' attempts to depict him as both.

Preparation
- Run through this activity yourself before doing it with the students.
- See pages 56-63 of the *CFH* for background information relevant to this activity.

Art
This activity uses the following artworks from *Beyond the Written Word:*
- *Wise Men from the East,* page 11
- *The Wedding at Cana,* page 13
- *Calming the Storm,* page 14
- *The Multiplication of Loaves and Fishes,* page 15
- *The Woman at the Well,* page 16
- *Peter Walks on Water,* page 17

1. Divide the class into pairs or triads. Assign each group one or two artworks to analyze. (If you feel the students would benefit from a sample analysis, use one piece of art to run through the activity with the whole class before assigning artwork to the small groups.)

2. After the students identify Jesus in the artwork(s), give them 5 to 10 minutes to discover and list the features that emphasize Jesus's humanity. Then have them list the features that point to Jesus's divinity. If necessary, spur the students' analysis by asking them to consider whether the following features appear in or affect the artwork:
- obvious features such as halos
- features or characteristics in Jesus that are similar to or different from the other people in the painting
- clothing or objects Jesus might be holding
- the artist's use of color or light
- the presence of heavenly figures such as angels
- Jesus's position in the painting (for example, central or off to the side)
- Jesus's position in the painting in relation to other people.

After the students complete their lists, ask them to decide whether they think each artist leans more toward depicting Jesus as human or as divine.

3. Ask a representative from each group to share that group's artwork(s) with the whole class, identifying which elements of the painting led the group to its conclusions about the artist's emphasis on humanity and divinity. After the sharing, ask the following questions:
- Do any of the pieces of art emphasize only Jesus's divinity or only his humanity? Would this be possible?

4. Invite the whole class to arrange the images in order from the most human portrayal of Jesus to the most divine depiction of Jesus. Ask the students to discuss the ways these paintings affect their understanding of the Incarnation.

Activity Extension

Invite the students to call to mind their usual image of Jesus. Ask them to notice whether it emphasizes Jesus's humanity or his divinity. Invite discussion about whether the students' own perceptions of Jesus seem to lean toward one side or the other and in what circumstances. Ask them this question:
- Does your own tendency to lean one way or the other limit the kind of messages you can receive about Jesus?

Invite discussion about whether the students might benefit from broadening their mental images of Jesus.

Recognizing Jesus After the Resurrection

In this activity, students look at how Jesus's disciples were able to see in a new way after Jesus rose from the dead. The students then compare those moments of recognition to similar moments of spiritual insight in their own lives.

Preparation
- Read or review Luke 24:13-35, the story of the disciples on the road to Emmaus.
- See pages 83-91 of the *CFH* for background information relevant to this activity.
- Have a Bible on hand.

Art
This activity focuses on *The Pilgrims of Emmaus*, on page 25 of *Beyond the Written Word*, and briefly uses other paintings in the book.

1. Ask the students to look at the painting *The Pilgrims of Emmaus* as you read Luke 24:13-35. (As on option, consider having three students act out the walk and the conversation in the Scripture passage.)

Afterward, ask these questions:
- How does the artist communicate the disciples' realization or recognition of who Jesus is?

- What is the relationship of light to awareness or knowledge? (Phrases such as "the light bulb went on" or "enlightenment" will likely surface.)

- In which way does awareness dawn on the disciples in the Emmaus story? Suddenly or gradually?

2. The disciples' new awareness of the resurrected Jesus would have shaped their whole understanding of Jesus's life, suffering, and death. Tell the students to imagine they are the two disciples from the story and have just been given *Beyond the Written Word*. In small groups, or as a whole class, have the students—while still imagining they are the disciples in the story— leaf through the book beginning with the last painting and moving backward. Tell them they are to pause at each painting, taking a moment to discuss how the painting enlightens them as they gaze at it. In this way, the students can experience the way that Jesus's followers saw his life differently after they understood the magnitude of his death and Resurrection.

3. Ask the students whether they have ever been surprised by a light-of-understanding experience similar to that of the disciples. Ask whether anyone has experienced a more gradual light of understanding. Finally, inquire whether any of the students feel that despite getting information about Catholicism and the Scriptures, they have yet to experience the light-bulb effect. In other words, they still struggle to make sense of their faith. Ask the students to share their experiences with the class if they are comfortable doing so.

Invite the students to keep their eyes and ears open at Mass and as they encounter the world. In other words, ask them to be present to their experiences because they never know when the shock of recognition will strike them.

4. Conclude the activity by noting how similar today's Catholics are to the disciples of Emmaus. Reinforce your remarks with these or similar words:
- In some ways, we remain in the dark about the mystery of who Jesus is, yet at the same time Jesus's revelation to us helps us recognize him properly when we look at his life and when we celebrate the sacraments today.

The Way to the Last Judgment

In this activity, students will examine two paintings. Using the first painting, they will become familiar with some of the elements of the Last Judgment. With the second painting, they will reflect on the relationship between the Last Judgment and our lives on earth.

Preparation
- Read or review Matthew 25:31-34.
- See pages 123-131 of the *CFH* for background information relevant to this activity.
- Have a Bible on hand.

Art
This activity uses the following artworks from *Beyond the Written Word:*
- *The Last Judgment,* page 30
- *The Ladder of Ascent,* page 29

1. Ask the students to look at *The Last Judgment* while you read Matthew 25:31-34 aloud, pausing after each line for discussion.

2. After you read each line, invite discussion about how the painting depicts the Scripture passage. For example, in verse 31, "in his glory," "angels," and "throne of his glory" are concrete images. Ask the students to name how and where each of the biblical references is depicted in the painting.

3. Have the students focus on the figures at Jesus's right hand and those at his left hand, and ask them to describe the differences between them. Record their answers on the board.

4. Now read Matthew 25:31-34 aloud, and then continue through verse 46. Ask the students to determine where the two groups sitting at Jesus's hands fit into the Gospel passage. (Are these people portrayed in the painting as living or dead?) Students will likely recognize that the people on either side of Jesus are dead and have already lived either as "the righteous" or as "the accursed."

5. Invite the students to turn to the painting *The Ladder of Ascent.* Tell them the painting depicts an event that takes place before death, before the final judgment. Take a couple of minutes to allow the students to identify or to point out the similarities, such as the following, between *The Ladder of Ascent* and *The Last Judgment:*
- Both have angels.
- Both have devil-like creatures.

- Jesus is portrayed in both.
- Both paintings have one group of "good" people and one group of "bad" people.

Next, ask the students to compare the two paintings, focusing their attention on the differences between the two groups of people in each painting. You should expect the students to list at least the following comparisons:

The Ladder of Ascent	*The Last Judgment*
• Jesus is at the top of a ladder.	• Jesus is sitting on a throne.
• The good people are climbing a ladder.	• The good people are praying quietly.
• More people are being added to the group of bad people below the ladder because the demons are pulling them off the ladder.	• The demons are not moving people from one group to the other.
• Jesus is sticking out of a hole in the sky.	• Jesus is big and central to the scene, instead of being in a corner of the sky.
• The angels are farther away from Jesus.	• The angels surround Jesus.
• The demons are using hooks and bows and arrows to grab the people on the ladder.	• The demons are using their tools only on the condemned.
• The bad people are still wearing clothes.	• The condemned are naked and vulnerable.
• The good people on the ladder look stressed.	• The saved are calm and peaceful.

Although there are many differences between the two paintings, highlight the following observations about the *The Ladder of Ascent:*

○ Jesus is reaching out to the people on the ladder rather than reigning on his throne as he is portrayed in *The Last Judgment.*

○ The people on the ladder, those that the demons have not yet snared, are active; they are doing something. Unlike the righteous who sit at Jesus's right hand in *The Last Judgment,* the people on the ladder are still alive and capable of choice.

○ The people the demons are pulling off the ladder aren't underground yet; they could try to escape the demons and go back to the bottom of the ladder to try again to reach Jesus.

6. Ask the students to connect the people on the ladder to the passage from Matthew about the Last Judgment. Where in the passage do these people appear? Ask the students how the ladder can be a metaphor for the way of life described in Matthew's Gospel.

7. Draw the students' attention again to *The Ladder of Ascent.* Ask them the following questions:
○ Where are the people on the ladder looking (toward whom or what are their faces pointed)? If we were to follow the example of those who are staying on the ladder, where should we keep our gaze?

- What do you notice about Jesus's posture in relation to the people on the ladder?

- Is Jesus holding his arms open only for the few people depicted in the painting or for all the people trying to stay on the ladder?

Activity Extension

This activity has focused on the black and the white, the judgment of the good and the bad. Sometimes that kind of clarity is necessary so we do not gloss over the difficulty of entering through the narrow gate. Nevertheless, pastoral practice requires that we also attend to our experience of living in the gray area that lies between the black and the white.

Direct the students' attention to *The Woman at the Well*, on page 16, and the *The Last Supper*, on page 20, of *Beyond the Written Word*. Ask the students to focus on Jesus's facial expressions and postures in the paintings. Ask them the following question:

- Does Jesus seem to be directing a judgmental look toward either the woman or Judas? [No.]

Point out to the students that both paintings depict a moment when it is clear that Jesus knows a sinner is present. Note that we know Jesus is aware that the woman has had five husbands and isn't actually married to her current one (see John 6:17-18), but Jesus entrusts her with carrying one of his most important teachings to others. Also point out that in *The Last Supper*, Jesus is breaking the bread just after announcing that he knows his betrayer. Mention that Judas is the one with the bag of money hidden behind his back but that Jesus isn't even looking at Judas; Jesus allows Judas to share in the first Eucharist.

These two paintings affirm the message of *The Ladder of Ascent*. As long as a person is alive and capable of making choices, he or she can hope for reconciliation with God and a restoration of the relationship of the mutual love God offers that the person might have rejected.

"We Believe in the Holy Spirit"

In this activity, students will look at two paintings to explore the experience of the Apostles at Pentecost as the Holy Spirit filled them. This activity provides the opportunity for thirteen students to "become" the painting.

Preparation

- Read or review Acts 2:1-42, the story of Pentecost.
- See pages 92-99 of the *CFH* for background information relevant to this activity.
- Think through the stage-management logistics before you attempt the activity. Also decide where the reenactment should take place and how you want to arrange seating to make it work. Try to find a place where it can be enacted under a bright light.
- Talk to your students' science teachers to find out how much the students have learned about the phenomena of light and heat: the visible spectrum and the invisible spectrum. If they do not have a general understanding that various wavelengths of light (radiation) are all around us, then modify step 2 accordingly, or do your best to give a brief overview of the concept yourself.

Art

This activity uses the following artworks from *Beyond the Written Word*:
- *The Descent of the Holy Ghost*, page 26
- *The Holy Spirit*, page 27

1. Invite the students to look at *The Descent of the Holy Ghost* and *The Holy Spirit*. Ask them to identify details the two paintings have in common (the rays of light and the tongues of fire). Ask them to share what they know about the relationship of symbolism of fire and light to the Holy Spirit.

2. Share the following ideas with the class in your own words:
- What do you know about wavelengths of light and radiation? Are you aware that even though we cannot see some wavelengths of light, such as infrared and ultraviolet, they are all around us? This is one of the reasons that light is such a good symbol for the Holy Spirit.

- Have you ever seen a laser beam as it is being used as a cutting tool on television or in a movie? Do the beams of light with flames at the end in *The Descent of the Holy Ghost* resemble a laser that causes some burning when it hits something? Do you think that the Holy Spirit had a similar effect on the Apostles during the event this painting depicts?

3. Now invite the students to focus their attention on *The Descent of the Holy Ghost*. Ask them to summarize the story of the Pentecost as shown in the painting. Read aloud Acts 2:1–8, then summarize the rest of the story. Tell the students they are going to reenact the event shown in the painting to help them explore how the Apostles and Mary might have felt when they experienced Pentecost.

4. Assign roles from among the people depicted in the painting to thirteen students. Give each student-actor a couple of minutes to study the gestures and expressions of her or his character. Set the stage to resemble the painting so that the students can begin to get into place. Invite them to get comfortable in their roles. Provide the following guided imagery for all the students:
- You are followers of Jesus, who was crucified six weeks ago. Jesus then came back and lived among you for a few weeks and, finally, a few days ago, was drawn up into heaven before your eyes.

- You are still not sure whether the authorities want to silence Jesus's followers, so you are living in some fear.

- You are not sure what to do now that Jesus is gone, so you are praying together until something happens to point the way.

Ask the thirteen actors to get into the exact positions their characters assume in the painting. You or some other student should stand outside the group and adjust the positions as needed. When everyone is in position, ask the actors to freeze, and if you have a bright light above the group, turn it on. Ask the actors to *be* their characters. Ask them to silently reflect on the following questions:
- What do you feel?

- What do you notice?

Ask the students who are not in the picture to also make observations of the living painting.

5. Give the actors a few moments in their positions, and then tell them it is okay to move again. Repeat the scene, if desired, so others can participate.

6. When the enactment is finished, invite the actors to report what they noticed while they were in the scene, and ask the observers to report what they noticed. Did the simulation allow them to see or understand the Holy Spirit in a new way? Invite the students to compare what they experienced in the simulation with the characteristics of the Holy Spirit they identified in steps 1 and 2. To create a parallel to real life, ask the students to consider the difference between witnessing the work of the Spirit in others versus personally experiencing the Spirit. Offer the following comment:

○ While words teach us something about the Spirit, visual imagery brings us yet a step further by giving color and shape to the unseen. Personal experience, however, fully enfleshes the experience.

One, Holy, Catholic, Apostolic

In this activity, students will explore the four marks of the Church by creating their own art.

This activity is based on the activity "Becoming the Religious Artist," on page 22 of this resource.

Ask students to make a work of art that reflects the four marks of the Church from the Creed. Use the steps from "Becoming the Religious Artist," and substitute the four marks of the Church whenever that activity speaks of the concept the student artists will create in visible form. Use handout 1-A, "Creating a Piece of Religious Art," to give the students the guidance they need to create an image that communicates the meaning of one of these marks.

Chapter 3

The Sacraments

Overview

The sacraments of the Catholic Church are visual and kinesthetic rituals rich in symbolism. The activities in this chapter invite you and your students to notice and explore aspects of several sacraments through art.

Activities

Symbols
- Finding the Symbols of the Mass

The Eucharist
- Jesus's Disciples
- Loaves and Fishes for the World

Penance and Reconciliation
- The Effects of Reconciliation

Marriage
- Matrimony, Creation, and Community
- The Marriage of Mary and Joseph

Additional Activity
- Taking a Field Trip

Finding the Symbols of the Mass

In this activity, students review the nature of symbols in the sacraments and then search for sacramental symbols and ritual gestures in the artworks in *Beyond the Written Word*.

Preparation
- Run through this activity ahead of time so that you can give hints to the students when they do the activity in class.
- See pages 146–149 of *The Catholic Faith Handbook for Youth (CFH)* for background information relevant to this activity.

Paintings

All paintings in *Beyond the Written Word* will be examined in this activity.

1. Talk about the meaning of the word *symbol* with the students, and review the nature of symbols in the seven sacraments. Focus on the fact that the Mass is composed of ritual and that because ritual is symbolic action, we can explore the meaning of the Mass through its rituals and symbols. Ask the students to identify some symbols and rituals from the Mass and explain their meanings.

2. Divide the class into small groups. Challenge the groups to each find as many symbolic pictures or gestures from the Mass in the paintings as possible. Some of the symbols and rituals the students find will include the following:
- The Wise Men bring their gifts to the altar just as we bring forward at the Offertory the gifts of bread and wine, the gifts of our own lives, and the collected money or food (*Wise Men from the East*, page 11).
- The community gathered in celebration is also present in the celebration of the Mass and is especially similar to the nuptial Mass (*The Wedding at Cana*, page 13).
- The disciples distribute bread to the people and the ministers today distribute the Eucharist at Communion (*The Multiplication of Loaves and Fishes*, page 15).
- The reverence of Jesus's followers when he is raising the bread in blessing and saying the words of consecration is mirrored in our own reverence as we participate in the Eucharistic prayer at Mass (*The Last Supper*, page 20).
- Jesus's blood on the white garment is the blood of Christ in the Eucharist (*Christ Crowned with a Crown of Thorns*, page 22).
- The symbol of the cross is present in the sign of the cross at Mass as well as in the crucifix on the altar (*Christ on the Cross*, page 23).
- Jesus holds the bread toward heaven to bless it as the priest does in the Mass (*The Pilgrims of Emmaus*, page 25).

After the students have found as many examples as possible, ask them to consider how much visual symbolism and ritual is in the Mass. Have them close their eyes and imagine what the Mass would be like if the priest and the congregation simply sat, without bows, processions, and the sign of the cross. How do these imagined changes help us understand the prevalence, significance, and effect of visual symbols and rituals within the Mass?

Jesus's Disciples

In this activity, the students insert modern followers as disciples of Jesus into the painting just as the painter included people of his own time. This activity is a good precursor to the next activity, "Loaves and Fishes for the World," because the painting emphasizes that part of our call as disciples is to feed those who are hungry. Both activities use the same painting.

Preparation
- Read or review John 6:1-15, the story about feeding the five thousand people.
- See chapter 18, "The Eucharist," of the *CFH* as background information for this activity.
- Have a Bible on hand.

Art

This activity uses *The Multiplication of Loaves and Fishes*, on page 15 of *Beyond the Written Word*.

1. Ask a student to read John 6:1–15.

2. Ask the students to identify the places in the painting where the artist used his imagination and included details that differ from the biblical account.

Invite the students to closely examine the clothing that various figures in the painting are wearing. Note that Jesus and the disciples are wearing clothes that Europeans of the artist's time traditionally thought Jesus would have worn. The people sitting on the ground, however, are in the clothing of late-medieval German-speaking people.

Ask the students this question:
- Why might the artist have included people of his own time rather than people of Jesus's time in the painting?

Suggest that artists often include people of their own time because the Bible is relevant in all times and places. The artist also likely wanted the people of his own time to see themselves as members of the crowd following Jesus.

3. Invite the students to work in small groups and to imagine they are working with a local artist who wants to reproduce *The Multiplication of Loaves and Fishes* with a present-time setting. The task of each group is to develop some advice for the artist about how to paint the people sitting on the ground. Tell the groups to record their main points on a piece of paper. The students should consider the ages of the people, their appearance, their clothing, their hair styles, their mood, and so on. Ask the students to think about what people look like who devotedly follow Jesus and listen to his talks. Students can portray the local community or the global community. Invite the groups to share with the class. Summarize the common themes.

4. Did any groups "paint" themselves into the picture? If not, invite the students to consider whether they would be among Jesus's followers. Ask them the following questions:
- Would they come to hear what Jesus had to say and to witness his miracles?

- Could they see themselves as disciples, actually helping Jesus feed the crowd? [If students cannot envision themselves this way, ask them to explain why.]

Loaves and Fishes for the World

In this activity, the students explore the relationship between the Eucharist and feeding hungry people. The previous activity was a good foundation for this activity.

Preparation
- Read or review John 6:1–15 and John 25–28,48–51, the story of feeding the five thousand people and its follow-up.
- See chapter 18, "The Eucharist," of the *CFH* as background for this activity.
- Have a Bible on hand.

Art

This activity uses *The Multiplication of Loaves and Fishes,* on page 15 of *Beyond the Written Word.* (If you did the previous activity with your students, begin at step 3.)

1. Ask a student to read aloud John 6:1–15 to the class.

2. Invite the students to examine the painting *The Multiplication of Loaves and Fishes.* Reread John 6:1–15 slowly and ask the students to mentally note parts of the story in the painting as you are reading. Then ask the students the following questions:
   - What of the biblical story do you see in the painting?

   - What is missing?

3. Point out that the painting shows the Apostles' handing out bread from the original few loaves while four baskets of bread are sitting at Jesus's feet. Note that telling several parts of one story in the same painting is a common technique that artists often use to convey the deeper meaning of a story. A piece of art also commonly tells a story at two levels simultaneously: the physical, or concrete, level and the spiritual level.

4. Pose these questions to the students:
   - On a symbolic level, why might the artist have included the baskets of leftover bread in the painting?

   - What might the leftover baskets of bread symbolize?

Students may suggest interpretations of this nature:
- The people who follow Jesus receive bread, and the bread is Jesus.
- Even though it appears there is not much food to start with, after the people receive this bread that is Jesus, the presence of Jesus increases. (The leftover bread symbolizes the increased presence of Jesus.)
- Followers of Jesus are supposed to do the work of God, and maybe the leftover bread will help them do this.

5. Return to the work of the Apostles, who are feeding the hungry people. Ask the class the following questions:
   - Who might the Apostles feed if they were among us today?

   - What are people hungry for in your own town or neighborhood today? [Offer this hint: People may be hungry for something other than food.]

6. Have the students form small groups and within their groups to ask one another this question:
   - What hungers do you witness in your own lives?

Have the groups develop lists of the hungers their members personally witness. Wander around and listen to their conversations. Gently encourage the students to recall their own experiences. For example, if they visit nursing homes, hospitals, or homeless shelters, they can talk about those experiences. If they focus on their own worlds, you should hear words such as *time, attention, love,* and *less stress.* Have the groups share their lists.

7. Invite the students to discern how the artist invites the viewer into an important sequence: first, the Apostles are fed by Jesus; then, the Apostles feed others with the abundant nature of Jesus's presence. Invite the groups to list the things that would feed the hungers they identified in step 6. Ask them to share their findings with the whole class.

Challenge the students to use one of the ideas generated in this step to try to feed one person physically or spiritually before the week is over. Remind the young people that they can feed others more abundantly if they attend Mass and are fed by the Eucharist.

Homework Idea

For homework, have students look at the lower half of the "Detail of the *Moone Cross*," on page 12 of *Beyond the Written Word,* and answer the following questions:

- What message might the image of the loaves and fishes have communicated to Irish peasants and monks in the mid-800s? (Remind the students that most of the people who saw the *Moone Cross* could not read the Bible but would have heard preaching about the story. The people would also have been poor and sometimes hungry, especially during the winter.)
- Do you think this simple carving would have been enough to remind those people of the biblical story of the loaves and fishes? What would those images have communicated to them, given their situation?
- Draw or describe a visual representation of the reading of the loaves and fishes that could be understood by anyone today, regardless of his or her reading ability. What parts of the story would you emphasize?

The Effects of Reconciliation

Learners will explore the effects of reconciliation with God that they experience in the sacrament of Penance and Reconciliation or individually with God for less serious sins.

Preparation

- Read or review Matthew 14:22-33.
- See pages 184-188 of the *CFH* for background information relevant to this activity.
- Have a Bible on hand.

Art

This activity uses the following artworks from *Beyond the Written Word:*
- *Peter Walks on Water*, page 17
- *The Penitent Saint Peter*, page 28
- *Calming the Storm*, page 14

1. Tell the students that they will examine three paintings so they can explore the steps a person takes from first committing a sin to finally becoming reconciled with God. People often find themselves in situations where they are vulnerable to sin. They often then sin, feel separated from God, and experience sorrow. Finally, they humbly return to and feel the peace of God.

2. Invite the students to turn to *Peter Walks on Water*. Read Matthew 14:22–33 to the students to review the story. Ask the students to name some adjectives that describe this painting. Record their suggestions on the board. Because the painting is somewhat chaotic and stormy, ask the students to suggest places in their own lives, or in the lives of others, that might have the same qualities (the beginning of lunch period, the halls between classes, taking a test, being at a party, and so on).

Suggest to them that storm and chaos can symbolize the often confusing, complex, chaotic situations of everyday life. When a lot is happening, when someone is encountering many people, or when physical or emotional risk is present, chaos is possible. Note that this kind of environment can tempt us more easily to sin.

Point to Peter in the painting. Remind the students that Peter walked on water while he was focused on Jesus. But at the moment Peter doubted Jesus, he started to sink. Have the students make four columns on a sheet of paper, labeling the first column "stormy situations" and the second column "potential sins."

3. Invite the students to turn to *The Penitent Saint Peter*. Ask them the following question:

- What is Peter's disposition?

Point out that Peter's sorrow suggests that he has separated himself from the will of God through sin, has recognized the sin, and is reflecting on how terrible it feels to be separated from God. Note also that in the painting, Peter has clearly moved past recognition to sorrow for the choices he made.

Remind the students that we know some of Peter's sins. Point out that sins, even seemingly small sins, separate us from God. Note also that Peter truly looks sorrowful in the painting. He is not making excuses for himself. He knows *he* chose to remove himself from his connection with God. Have the students label the third column on their paper "separation and sorrow."

4. Invite the students to turn to *Calming the Storm* (see Matthew 3:23–27, Mark 4:35–41, Luke 8:22–25). Suggest that this painting symbolizes how dramatically the storm can be calmed and the separation bridged when we ask for God's forgiveness and receive it. Note that this artist included both the storminess and the calm in the painting so the difference would be more emphatic. The calming of the storm of wind and waves symbolizes the inner peace we experience after reconciliation. With inner calm, even in the midst of otherwise stormy situations, we are able to make good decisions. Have the students label the fourth column on their paper "calm."

5. Invite the students to form groups of three or four. Then instruct the groups to each make a list of the potential stormy situations its members encounter in the world. Give them these directions:

- List several stormy situations in column 1.

- For each situation, list a few of the possible sins, from ignoring a friend to committing a serious sin, in column 2.

- In column 3, next to each sin, explain how that sin is a choice to separate oneself from God.

○ Finally, in column 4, describe the calm that results for each situation after the person reconciles with God. [What does the situation look like when there is no storminess?]

6. Invite the groups to share from their lists with the whole class. Conclude by asking the students to consider how much stronger they would be if they encountered temptation from a position of calm. Note that the Church provides the sacrament of Penance and Reconciliation to offer us peace when we have separated ourselves from God through serious sin. For less serious sin, we can express sorrow for our sins and ask for God's forgiveness to achieve greater peace.

Matrimony, Creation, and Community

In this activity, students will explore the relationships between the married couple, Creation, and the community. This activity is naturally followed by the activity "The Marriage of Mary and Joseph," but the two activities can also be done as standalones.

Preparation
- Read or review John 2:1-11 and Genesis 2:15—3:7. While reading them, focus on three elements of the passages: the couple, the community, and the presence of God's gifts.
- See chapter 20, "Sacraments at the Service of Communion," of the *CFH* for background information relevant to this activity.
- Have a Bible on hand.

Art
This activity uses the following artworks from *Beyond the Written Word:*
- *The Wedding at Cana,* page 13
- *Adam and Eve,* page 10

1. Ask the students to turn to *The Wedding at Cana.* Ask volunteers to retell the story in the painting. Fill in missing details or read John 2:1-11 aloud.

2. Invite the students to notice the details of the wedding. First, have them locate Jesus, Mary, and the bride and groom, who are sitting under the awning. The groom is in blue and white, and the bride is in pink. Then guide the students through the painting using the following questions (share with the students the bracketed interpretive information if they do not suggest the ideas themselves):
- What is different about the couple as compared with everyone else? [They are sitting on chairs or a bench while others are sitting on the ground, they are protected from the sun by an awning, or the musicians are facing them.] What is the symbolism of these differences? [The couple's importance.]
- Why do you think the bride and groom are not facing each another? [They are facing the guests, the village, and the feast going on in front of them. Marriage has an important community dimension. The presence of the community emphasizes that the couple's love is to be shared outside of their families. The couple wants community support of the union, and the community wants to give it.]

- What might the quantity of jars and the exceptional quality of the wine symbolize about marriage? [The abundance of God's gifts is made available to married couples as they go forth into the world together.]

3. Ask the students to compare the symbolism of posture and place within the painting with the symbolism of the elements of the sacrament of Matrimony. Ask them the following questions:
- In weddings you have witnessed, how is the couple set apart as especially important people?

- In the sacrament of Matrimony, when does the couple face each other? What is the role of the larger community during the ritual?

- Why does the Church refuse to celebrate the sacrament of Matrimony for a couple without the community present?

- How is God's grace for a married couple similar to the wine from the story at Cana?

4. Ask the students to turn their attention to *Adam and Eve.* Invite volunteers to retell the story that the painting depicts. Fill in any missing pieces of the story or read Genesis 2:15—3:7 aloud. Remind the students that Adam and Eve were the first married couple.

5. Discuss the painting and related themes by asking the following questions:
- Which gifts surround the couple on all sides? [The gifts of God's abundance in Creation—plants and animals—are there to bless and support the couple—Adam and Eve.]

- To what do Adam and Eve pay attention in the midst of this abundance? [They look at the serpent and the tree from which they are not supposed to eat.]

- What do you think when you see someone focusing on something negative, something that completely overlooks the gifts and abundance around them? [Sometimes people focus on what they cannot have instead of appreciating the good that is around them. It appears that such people lack gratitude.]

- What are some of God's abundant gifts in marriage? [God's grace, the gift of married love, and the gift of children should be among the answers.]

- What are signs you see that a married couple appreciates and receives God's gifts? rejects God's gifts?

6. In closing, summarize some of the observations the students have made about the ideal way the couple in the first painting relates to the community and God's other gifts to them and the disordered way the couple in the second painting relates to God and God's gifts. Ask them what can be learned from the contrast.

The Marriage of Mary and Joseph

Mary and Joseph model the way couples can handle hardship and challenge. The "Matrimony, Creation, and Community" activity is a good foundation for this activity but not necessary in order to complete it.

Preparation

- See chapter 20, "Sacraments at the Service of Communion," of the *CFH* for background information relevant to this activity.
- Read or review Luke 2:1-7, the story of Jesus's birth, and Matthew 2:1-12,13-23, the visit of the Wise Men.
- Have a Bible on hand.

Art

This activity uses the following artworks from *Beyond the Written Word:*
- *Wise Men from the East*, page 11
- Detail of the *Moone Cross* (focus on the top half: the flight into Egypt), page 12
- *The Wedding at Cana*, page 13

1. Ask the students to turn their attention to *The Wise Men from the East*. Invite volunteers to retell the story that the painting depicts. Fill in missing details, or read aloud Luke 2:1-7 and Matthew 2:1-12.

2. Invite the students to look at aspects of Mary and Joseph's married life in this painting. Ask them the following questions:
- What kind of environment are Joseph, Mary, and Jesus in? [The environment includes a rough stable with straw, animals, Joseph's plain clothes.]

- What would be the logistics of taking care of a newborn baby in that environment? [Such a task would be challenging.]

- Compare this painting to *The Wedding at Cana*. With whom would you compare the Wise Men? [The Wise Men represent the community; it does not matter that they are not friends and family.]

- What do the Wise Men's gifts to Mary and Joseph symbolize in the couple's difficult circumstances? [Such gifts symbolize the abundance of God's gifts.]

Offer the following comment:
- God gifts us through the community, and through the community, we come to see how God blesses us.

3. Ask the students to turn to the "Detail of the *Moone Cross*." Tell the students to focus on the top part of the art, which portrays Joseph's leading the donkey that carries Mary, who is holding Jesus, during the family's flight into Egypt. Ask for a volunteer to retell the story. Fill in missing details, or read aloud Matthew 2:13-23.

4. Guide them with these questions about the *Moone Cross*:
- Do Joseph and Mary have it any easier in the *Moone Cross* scene than the couple in *The Wise Men from the East* or in *The Wedding at Cana*? [No.]

- Where are God's abundant gifts in the *Moone Cross*? [They are harder to see.]

- Where is the community? [It is not visible.]

- Did God abandon Mary, Joseph, and Jesus? [No, God never abandons us even if it seems that way.]

Conclude the activity with these observations:

- God promises abundant gifts and community to a couple in marriage. The couple experience a sense of community in their own relationship because they make gifts of themselves to each other, and they work as a team. Mary and Joseph likely shared the gifts of love and companionship with the people they were thrown into community with during their journey and when they arrived in Egypt. All couples can ask for the support of the community. The couple can find the abundance of God's gifts in the people they meet, as they can within their own marriage ties.

Homework Idea

Assign the students the task of interviewing a married couple they know. They are to ask the couple about the importance of community and of God's gifts during their marriage.

Taking a Field Trip

Take the students to a chapel or a church. Using the skills you and the students have learned, do the following activities with the students:

- Explore the art that decorates the tabernacle, the altar, the baptismal font, the windows, and the stations of the cross.
- Have the students identify images and symbols that go with different sacraments.
- Invite the students to stand in the entryway of the Church and assess what the space communicates to them visually. Ask them to consider what they are learning about the community as they look around. Ask them to identify any symbols or visual pieces that could better communicate the nature of the parish or community.
- Again ask the students to gaze around the entryway. Ask them to notice whether there are any visual indicators that young people are an important part of the parish. Ask them to identify why they think young people are important to the parish. If no symbols of youth involvement are evident, ask the students what symbols would make the parish welcoming to young people.

Morality

Chapter 4

Overview

Living a moral life has been part of being a disciple of Jesus Christ since he walked the earth. Artists have expressed what this struggle to live a moral life has meant to them and, in their art, have offered support for those who also struggle. The activities in this chapter are designed to help the students think about morality and live better lives.

Activities

- Disciple Hunt
- The Good Samaritan: Morality in Parables
- Jesus the Teacher
- Jesus and Mary: Models of Fortitude

Disciple Hunt

In this activity, the students will look through *Beyond the Written Word* for the artworks that best represent, in their view, the descriptions of discipleship listed on handout 4, "Disciple Hunt." The answers listed at the end of this activity include the name of the artwork, its page number, and a brief explanation.

Preparation
- Depending on whether the students will work as individuals or in groups, make enough copies of handout 4 so that each student or group has one. Look through the answer list ahead of time.
- See pages 206–215 of *The Catholic Faith Handbook for Youth (CFH)* for background information relevant to this activity.

Art

All the artworks in *Beyond the Written Word* are used in this activity.

1. Distribute handout 4 to the students, or have the class form groups and give each group one copy of the handout.

2. Tell the students that each quality of a good disciple listed on the handout is evident in an artwork in *Beyond the Written Word*. The students' mission is to search the artworks for a disciple or disciples exhibiting one of the good discipleship qualities listed on the handout. They are then to list the artwork and its page number in the appropriate space. Give the students 10 minutes for this search.

3. Go over the answers in class with the students, using the answers to fuel a discussion about why each quality on the handout is an element of discipleship. Invite the students to offer suggestions on how the acts of discipleship depicted in the artwork translate into actions they can use as disciples in today's world.

Answers to handout 4

a. *The Pilgrims of Emmaus*, page 25. (The two disciples open themselves to the light of the truth that shines on them after they had walked in darkness.)

b. Detail of the *Moone Cross*, page 12. (Mary and Joseph uproot the family in order to flee to Egypt.)

c. or k. *The Good Samaritan*, page 18, or *The Good Samaritan (After Delacroix)*, page 19. (The Samaritan helps the suffering man in spite of the social pressure to avoid him.)

d. *The Ladder of Ascent*, page 29. (Those on the ladder are on the path to God in spite of challenges; the demons are trying to pull them off.)

e. *The Penitent Saint Peter*, page 28. (Peter weeps in sorrow and repentance for his sins and failures.)

f. *Wise Men from the East*, page 11. (These men have traveled far or have gone the extra mile to worship the new King.)

g. *The Woman at the Well*, page 16. (This woman engages in conversation with Jesus and listens to his word, even though others would consider Jesus's talking to her to be scandalous.)

h. *The Multiplication of Loaves and Fishes*, page 15. (The disciples do the work of God to help the world by distributing loaves and fishes to the people assembled.)

i. *Calming the Storm*, page 14. (The frightened disciples turn to Jesus in a time of crisis.)

j. *Peter Walks on Water*, page 17. (With faith, Peter can walk on water.)

k. or c. *The Good Samaritan*, page 18, or *The Good Samaritan (After Delacroix)*, page 19. (The good Samaritan interrupts his journey so he can help the man in need.)

l. *Christ on the Cross*, page 23. (Jesus's mother Mary and the others endure this horror even though they cannot yet see the good to come out of it.)

m. *The Descent of the Holy Ghost*, page 26. (The Apostles and Mary gather to pray even though they are afraid the authorities will come after Jesus's followers.)

n. *The Last Supper*, page 20. (Jesus has just announced that one of the Apostles will betray him, but the Apostles are reverent and respectful as Jesus blesses the bread.)

o. *The Wedding at Cana*, page 13. (The couple commit their love to community by being married in the midst of the community.)

The Good Samaritan: Morality in Parables

The students will compare two interpretations of the good Samaritan parable and find both a personal and a social perspective on the story.

Preparation

• Read or review Luke 10:25-37, the parable of the good Samaritan and the circumstances that prompt Jesus to tell the story.

• Read the background material on the two paintings in appendix 1, "More About the Art," and be prepared to share it with the students.

• Have some rulers and calculators on hand for step 2.

• Have a Bible on hand.

Art

This activity uses the following artworks from *Beyond the Written Word:*

• *The Good Samaritan*, page 18

• *The Good Samaritan (After Delacroix)*, page 19

1. Invite the students to turn to the two paintings in *Beyond the Written Word* that depict the story of the good Samaritan. Ask the students to examine those pictures while you or a student reads Luke 10:25-37 aloud. (Before the reading, remind the students that a Levite was another Jewish temple official of that time). Ask the students to make a mental note of which of the two paintings they are most drawn to as they listen to the reading.

2. Invite the students to do a little math. Ask them to estimate how much of the Arellano painting is taken up by the figures of the Samaritan and the injured man and how much of the Van Gogh painting is taken up by those same figures. Tell them they can arrive at their estimates either by imagining a grid over each painting or by using rulers and calculators. (The figures take up a little more than one-tenth of the Arellano painting and one-half of the Van Gogh. To put it another way, the two figures make up only 10 percent of Arellano's painting and about 50 percent of Van Gogh's).

Ask the students to speculate whether the artists' use of differing amounts of space is significant. Does the amount of space the artist gives to one element of a story indicate how he or she interprets the story? Some of the students' answers may suggest that Van Gogh thought the size element was more important than did Arellano. Point out that the Arellano painting is a wide-angle shot of the big picture, while the Van Gogh painting is a close-up shot of one part of the story.

3. Ask the students to look at the two paintings again. Tell them to list the differences between the two paintings. Invite them to work in groups if they wish. Tell the students they are looking for elements present in Arellano's painting but absent in Van Gogh's and for the details they see in Van Gogh's but cannot see in Arellano's.

4. While the students compile their lists, make two columns on the board. Write "Present Only in Arellano's painting" as the heading of one column and "Present Only in Van Gogh's painting" as the heading of the other column. After the students have had a few minutes to look at the paintings and compile their lists, invite them to suggest items from their lists to be put in one column or the other. If they seem stuck, draw their attention to the landscape, the animals, the people on the road, the Samaritan, and the injured man. (For more ideas, see "How to Compare Images of the Same Biblical Story" on page 210.) The students should come up with all or some of the observations from, as well as additions to, the lists in the following chart. If necessary, ask the students leading questions to help them identify elements.

Present only in Arellano's painting

- Three holy people are on the road.
- The holy people look like late twentieth-century Catholics instead of Jewish people from Jesus's time.
- It is hard to tell where they are looking; they might be looking back at the two men.
- The people's clothes stand out against the landscape.
- There is a lot of land with trees.
- It is a beautiful place.
- The Samaritan's animal is a donkey.
- The donkey is not wearing fancy equipment.
- The road seems to lead to a far-off town.
- There is a mountain or volcano in the background.
- Neither the injured man nor the Samaritan can be seen clearly, so not much can be said about them.

Present only in Van Gogh's painting

- There is one holy man on the road.
- The holy man has his back to the injured man and the Samaritan.
- The holy man's clothes blend in with the landscape.
- The Samaritan's animal is a horse.
- The horse has nice equipment.
- The injured man can be seen clearly and is obviously helpless.
- The Samaritan can be seen clearly and seems muscular and capable.
- The road leads deeper into the mountains.
- The landscape is rough and plain.

5. Have the students review the lists on the board. Ask them as a group to rate on a scale of 1 (least important) to 10 (most important) how important the holy man is in the Van Gogh painting. (Record the students' rating next to the first reference to the holy man on the list.)

Repeat the process with the landscape, the horse, and the details of the injured man and the Samaritan. The students should be expected to give a low rating for the holy man and the landscape , a higher rating for the horse, and an even higher rating for the injured man and the Samaritan.

6. Repeat the rating process for the same features (holy people, landscape, animal, injured man, the Samaritan) in Arellano's painting. The students should be expected to give a low rating for the holy people and the animal, and a higher rating for the injured man, the Samaritan, and the landscape. The latter three features could be similarly rated. Compare the Van Gogh ratings with the Arellano ratings, and make a statement that summarizes the students' observations about the relative importance of these elements to the artists.

7. Ask the students why two artists might read the same story and paint it so differently. Note that those differences might make more sense to the students if they knew a little bit more about the artists. Share the following information with them:

○ Van Gogh painted *The Good Samaritan (After Delacroix)* while he was in an asylum. The year before committing himself to the asylum, Van Gogh had cut off part of his left ear and had suffered a mental breakdown. When he painted *The Good Samaritan*, his ear injury had healed, but he was still having trouble with what some today think was a form of epilepsy.

○ Arellano was a poor Nicaraguan during the war between the Sandinistas and the Contras in the late 1970s and early 1980s. The war in Nicaragua, a rich and beautiful land, was being fought, in part, because foreign companies owned the land and the people of Nicaragua had nothing. The people suffered before and during the war. Priests, nuns, and bishops often were unsure which side to support. Some people got angry when they thought the priests, nuns, and bishops were not helping the people.

Ask the students whether the biographical information about the artists affects the students' interpretation of the paintings. If necessary, point out that the bandage on the injured man's head in the Van Gogh painting partly covers his left ear and that the three people on the road in Arellano's painting are a priest, a nun, and a bishop. Ask the students to summarize why they think the artists painted their works the way they did and what message each tried to convey.

8. Take the lesson one step further by making these comments:

○ No one would disagree that the story of the good Samaritan is about loving one's neighbor.

○ Personal circumstances will influence the way a person interprets what it means to love one's neighbor.

○ Some people will understand what it means to love one's neighbor from an individualistic or personal perspective. Others will take a political or social view. Neither approach is incorrect.

○ The Bible gives us moral guidance both in our personal lives and in our public or political lives.

Activity Extension

Because the students have just assessed two artistic versions of the good Samaritan story, the stage is set for them to create their own work of art as described in the activity "Becoming the Religious Artist," on page 22 This activity will help the students decide whether they want their art to have a personal or a social and political point of view. Their next step will be to consider how to make the story of the good Samaritan appealing, relevant, layered, and communicative to a modern-day audience.

After students have completed their artworks, allow enough time for them to discuss the issues they thought important enough to represent in their art.

Jesus the Teacher

In this activity, the students see that Jesus's invitation to relationship and his gift of living water constitute the real path to moral life.

Preparation

- Read or review John 4:1-30, the story of Jesus and the Samaritan woman at the well.
- Have a Bible on hand.

Art

This activity uses *The Woman at the Well* on page 16 of *Beyond the Written Word*.

1. Prepare the students for the exercise by asking their opinions on the following two questions. Record summaries of their answers on the board.

  ○ How does Jesus invite us into a relationship with him today?

  ○ How do virtues and vices help or hinder our relationship with Jesus?

2. Ask the students to turn their attention to *The Woman at the Well*. Read John 4:1-30 aloud. Ask these questions to help the students analyze the painting:

  ○ Describe the setting. [Well, trees, stone steps, wall]

  ○ Why does the woman come to this place? [To get water]

3. Invite the students to look at the painting and describe Jesus's facial expression and posture. Point out that Jesus appears to be making a gesture with his right hand that is intended to calm the woman. Ask the students the following questions:

  ○ Does Jesus look judgmental or threatening?

  ○ Has the artist painted Jesus larger than the woman or in a position above the woman?

  ○ How does Jesus come across overall?

  ○ Does this image surprise, challenge, or reassure you?

4. Have the students return their attention to the painting, this time focusing on the woman. They already know from the reading that the woman is living with a man to whom she is not married. Ask the students these questions:

- On what does she seem most focused?

- What does her position—leaning back, away from Jesus as they speak with each other—suggest?

- Does she look willing to put aside what she is doing so she can pay closer attention to him?

- Do the story and the painting give us a sense of the kind of relationship the woman and Jesus had at the end of their encounter?

5. Summarize the students' insights. Offer the following comments:

- Jesus offers us living water and a relationship with him. Just as in this story, the presence of Jesus and his loving invitation to us encourage us to live in new ways.

- The moral life is so much more than the sum of following many rules. The moral life is best lived in relationship with Jesus. Jesus invited the woman into a relationship with him even though she was living contrary to the law. Jesus meets us where we are—just as he met the woman—and his love for us enables us to live with greater virtue.

Jesus and Mary: Models of Fortitude

In this activity, students will examine Mary and Jesus in three types of situations, each of which is an example of a different kind of fortitude. The activity is in three parts—each one illustrative of one kind of fortitude. You can choose to do one, two, or all three parts.

Preparation

- Read and review Matthew 26:36—27:61; Mark 14:32—15:47; Luke 22:39—23:56; and John, chapters 18 and 19 (the stories of the Passion and the Crucifixion) and Acts 2:1-13 (the Pentecost).
- Read through the activity ahead of time, and decide whether you want the students to work individually or in groups.
- Read pages 296-297 of the *CFH* for background information relevant to the activity.
- Have a Bible on hand.

Art

This activity uses the following artworks from *Beyond the Written Word:*
- *Christ Crowned with a Crown of Thorns*, page 22
- *Christ on the Cross*, page 23
- Detail from *Mystic Crucifixion*, page 24
- *The Descent of the Holy Ghost*, page 26

Before examining one or more of the models of fortitude, invite the students to discuss the meaning of *fortitude*. Suggest that they use their dictionaries, their morality textbooks, or other sources. Tell them this activity will give them a chance to examine the fortitude of people who find themselves in the following three circumstances: experiencing personal pain and suffering, feeling powerless when faced with someone else's pain and suffering, and leading those who are experiencing pain or suffering.

Part A: Fortitude: Experiencing Personal Pain and Suffering

1. Invite the students (individually or in groups) to turn to *Christ Crowned with a Crown of Thorns*. Ask them to consider Jesus's situation as the artist has portrayed it. Point out that Jesus's hands are not bound, that the soldier is protecting his own hands by using a sword or spear to push the crown onto Jesus's head, and that several soldiers seem to be taunting or otherwise abusing Jesus.

Have the students spend a few minutes examining the painting. Ask them to think of contemporary situations that resemble the Crucifixion to a greater or lesser degree. Invite them to share those situations; record them on the board. (The list might include prisoners being abused, children being held hostage in a school, starving children around the world, forcing an intoxicated person to do things he or she would not do while sober, and students teasing or taunting other students in school.) If the students do not mention any school scenarios, ask them whether such situations have occurred in the school.

Invite the students to turn their attention to *Christ on the Cross*. Mention that Jesus is demonstrating fortitude in the face of his pain and suffering and that the Gospel of Luke refers to Jesus's calling on his Father to forgive those who arrested and crucified him.

2. Next, ask the students to focus their attention on Jesus in the painting. Remind them that Jesus is fully human and fully divine. Ask the students the following questions in your own words:

- What human feelings might Jesus be experiencing?

- What would be going through your mind if you were in his place? [Encourage the students to tap into the feelings they might have if someone were doing that to them.]

- What might Jackie Chan do if he were in Jesus's place? [Have the students share; write some of their thoughts on the board.]

- Does Jesus look as though he is having any of these thoughts? If so, does it appear that he is going to act on them?

- When we compare the human response to such suffering with Jesus's response, what do we learn about fortitude?

Point out that Jesus shows fortitude by having the strength and the courage to keep loving his tormenters, even though he is enduring human suffering at their hands.

Part B: Fortitude: Witnessing Someone Else's Pain and Suffering

1. Ask the students to look at the painting *Christ on the Cross*. Draw their attention to Mary, who is dressed in blue, and the other women gathered in front of Jesus as he hangs on the cross. The women are witnessing a wrong but are powerless to stop it. Note that Mary, of course, knows that the wrong being done to Jesus is undeserved.

Invite the students to study the painting again, this time to brainstorm a list of contemporary situations in which people feel powerless to stop an injustice they are witnessing. (The list might include knowing about political prisoners, being a passenger in a car pulled over because of racial profiling, witnessing a teacher or coach treat a student unfairly, watching someone become addicted to drugs or alcohol, knowing that a friend who is being abused will not seek help, and witnessing the torment of someone at school.) Record their scenarios on the board. If the students do not raise situations that arise in school, ask them whether such circumstances exist in the school.

2. Invite the students to focus again on Mary in the painting. Note that although other women are supporting Mary, she appears to be more emotionally involved in the event than they are. Have the students examine for a moment the detail from *Mystic Crucifixion*. Ask them to compare the demeanor of Mary, who is wrapped in her blue cloak, in *Christ on the Cross* with that of Mary Magdalene, who is almost spilling out of her red cloak, in *Mystic Crucifixion*. Ask the students which of the two women exhibit fortitude. If the students select only one Mary as having fortitude, ask them why. Invite another round of brainstorming on how Mary, Jesus's mother, is an example for those who find themselves in one of the situations listed on the board. Invite sharing.

Part C: Fortitude: Leading Those Who Are Experiencing Pain or Suffering

1. Invite the students to turn to *The Descent of the Holy Ghost* on page 26. Draw the students' attention to Mary, the mother of Jesus, and note that the artist has put her in the center of the Apostles in the Pentecost scene. (If necessary, review the story of Pentecost with the students.)

Here, Mary's position in the center portrays her as a pillar of strength, a stable force for the Apostles during the difficult days after Jesus's Ascension. Ask the students to brainstorm what kinds of contemporary situations resemble this scene, situations in which a person whose demeanor and characteristics may make her or him seem out of place but whose true leadership shows. Record their suggestions on the board. (The list might include a quiet prayerful protest outside an abortion clinic, an invitation to reflection at a heated student government meeting, a quiet transformation of a potentially destructive party into a respectable fun event, and a diplomatic effort to defuse an emotionally charged situation.) If the students do not suggest school-related examples, ask them whether such situations occur in the school.

2. Invite the students to again focus on Mary in *The Descent of the Holy Ghost*. Point out the subtle difference between the openness of Mary's raised arms and the defensiveness of the Apostles' arms held close to their bodies. Invite another round of brainstorming about how Mary's fortitude in this situation can inspire a person who leads suffering people. Invite sharing among the whole group. Ask the students if there are other ways they might portray of person of fortitude.

Closing: Fortitude: Examining Your Own

Invite the students to notice that in all three of these paintings, fortitude is evident in the postures of Jesus and Mary. Invite the students to become aware of their own postures at this moment in their lives. Ask questions like the following:

- Are you quietly enduring a beating such as Jesus endured?

- Are you standing firm in the face of suffering you are witnessing?

- Are you open to what the Holy Spirit has to offer?

- Are you able to discern when to quietly endure and stand firm and when to ask the Spirit for guidance on how to right the wrongs?

Challenge the students to become aware of their postures in the various situations in which they find themselves over the next couple of days.

Homework Idea

Invite the students to write several paragraphs about how they think the news media and the entertainment industries would handle a situation in which someone faced oppression, such as Jesus and Mary did. Tell them to consider the following questions:

- Would the news media be more likely to report a situation involving a person who reacted with violence or one involving a person who reacted with love and fortitude?

- Would the television or film industry be more likely to produce a program or film about a person reacting with violence or about a person reacting with love and fortitude?

- What about the music industry?

Disciple Hunt

For each quality of discipleship listed below, find a painting that portrays a disciple or group of disciples that best fits that quality and write the title of the painting on the line provided in the right-hand column.

Quality of discipleship

a. Being open to the light of truth

b. Uprooting their lives for the sake of God

c. Acting against social norms on the compassionate love God has given

d. Trying to stay on the path to God in spite of risks

e. Repenting sins and shortcomings

f. Going the extra mile to worship God

g. Listening to God's word despite social pressure

h. Doing the work of God to help the world

i. Turning to God in times of crisis

j. Demonstrating faith despite fear

k. Interrupting one's own plans when the needs of others demand

l. Trusting, when faced with horror, that God's plan may be beyond human understanding

m. Nourishing spiritual practices through prayer even when the world seems to be closing in

n. Celebrating God's goodness even when it is clear that not everything is good

o. Committing the gifts of love and abundance to God's service in the community

Painting

_____

_____

_____

_____

_____

_____

_____

_____

_____

_____

_____

_____

_____

_____

_____

Chapter 5

Prayer

Overview

Art facilitates prayer in many ways. This chapter's activities are designed to teach about prayer rather than to facilitate it.

Activities

- Prayers for All Occasions
- Prayers of Praise
- Prayers of Thanksgiving
- Prayer in Times of Hardship
- Prayers of Petition

Prayers for All Occasions

In this activity, students will use Bible stories to help them see that prayer is appropriate in every circumstance.

Preparation

- Read the background information for each of the nine paintings used in this activity.
- Be prepared to paraphrase the relevant Bible stories if the students are not familiar with them.
- See pages 304-313 and 343-344 in *The Catholic Faith Handbook for Youth (CFH)* for background information relevant to this activity.
- Have a Bible on hand.

Art

This activity uses the following artworks from *Beyond the Written Word*:

- Detail from *Mystic Crucifixion*, page 24
- *Peter Walks on Water*, page 17
- *Gethsemane: "If it is possible, may this cup be taken from me."* page 21
- *Calming the Storm*, page 14
- *Christ on the Cross*, page 23
- *The Penitent Saint Peter*, page 28
- *The Pilgrims of Emmaus*, page 25
- *Wise Men from the East*, page 11
- *The Last Judgment*, page 30

1. Invite the students to suggest life experiences that call for prayer. List their suggestions on the board.

2. Tell the students that prayer occurs in a number of Bible stories. Explain that they will view paintings that depict some of those prayer moments and will learn what the Bible teaches about appropriate occasions for prayer.

3. Ask the students to turn to the first artwork in the following list. Draw their attention to the relevant parts of the image. Offer the following comments and questions listed for each artwork. Record the students' answers on the board. The responses in parentheses can serve as additions to student answers or as prompts. Repeat the process with each artwork listed.

- Detail from *Mystic Crucifixion* (see John 19:25)
  - Notice that Mary Magdalene, shown grasping the foot of the cross on which Jesus has been crucified, is talking to an angel. Did the angel come because Mary had been praying? If so, why had Mary been praying? [Sadness, grief, loss]

- *Peter Walks on Water* (see Matthew 14:28-31)
  - As he sinks, Peter yells, "Lord, save me!" (verse 30). What causes Peter to utter this prayer? [Fear]

- *Gethsemane: "If it is possible, may this cup be taken from me."* (see Matthew 26:39)
  - Jesus is looking up to his heavenly Father and praying because he knows his arrest is imminent. What kind of emotion might Jesus be experiencing for him to utter the words that are the title of the painting? [Fear, apprehension]

- *Calming the Storm* (see Matthew 8:23-27)
  - Notice the disciples near Jesus. They are reaching up to him, asking to be saved. What kind of situation are they in? What caused their panic? [The storm, chaos, confusion, helplessness]

- *Christ on the Cross* (see Matthew 27:46 and Mark 15:34)
  - Jesus could not be in a worse situation, but he says, "My God, my God, why have you forsaken me?" This is the first line of Psalm 22, a prayer of hope and trust in God's goodness. What do you imagine are Jesus's thoughts in this situation? [Knowing that God will come through for him]

- *The Penitent Saint Peter* (see Matthew 26, Mark 14:72, and Luke 22:62)
  - Peter is crying and praying. Matthew, Mark, and Luke tell us that Peter, who had considered himself faithful, wept when he realized he had denied Jesus. Numerous writers in the early Church noted that Peter cried over his sins every night. What might be motivating Peter's praying in this painting? [Desire for forgiveness, plea for help to sin less.]

- *The Pilgrims of Emmaus* (see Luke 22:62)
  - Jesus is holding up the piece of bread, toward his Father. What feelings might be motivating him to pray?

- *Wise Men from the East* (see Matthew 2:11)
  - The wise men are kneeling before Jesus to praise him. What might we do when we encounter something sacred or awesome? [Praise and reverence for God]

- *The Last Judgment* (see Matthew 25:31-45)
  - Notice that the people at Jesus's right hand are praying. They are already dead and have been judged to be righteous. Why might they still be praying? [Praise, gratitude, habit of prayer even after death]

4. Invite the students to compare their list of occasions for prayer from step 1 with the list generated from the Bible passages in step 3. Ask them the following questions:
  - Would you add any occasions for prayer from the biblical list to your personal list of occasions or reasons for prayer?

  - What are some other examples of people praying in the Bible?

Activity Extension

Invite the students to think about their regular activities and to make a list of three occasions in their lives when they do not pray but might in the future.

Prayers of Praise

In this activity, students will analyze what it means to respond with praise to God's presence and greatness. Because you will be drawing answers from the students, try to use their own language throughout the activity whenever possible.

Preparation
- Read or review Matthew 2:1-12. Be prepared to read it to the class or have a student read it.
- See pages 320-322 of the *CFH* for background information relevant to this activity.

Art

This activity uses *Wise Men from the East,* on page 11 of *Beyond the Written Word.*

1. Have the students turn to *Wise Men from the East.* Ask them to describe what the Wise Men are doing. Write their observations on the board. (Responses could include kneeling, giving gifts, and bowing of heads.)

2. Ask the students to describe what each gesture or action might symbolize. (Responses could include such concepts as reverence, homage, honor, and praise, although the students might not use those exact words.)

3. Invite the students to reflect on and to describe how the Wise Men might have felt as they knelt and bowed their heads before this baby and presented him with gifts.

4. Read Matthew 2:1–12 aloud or have a student do so. After the reading, ask the students to describe the spiritual journey that the Wise Men took that culminated in the awe-filled reverence they offered Jesus. Note that when the Wise Men felt the call, they could have chosen either to respond or to not respond. Point out that they went on a journey in response to their call.

After listing the students' answers, offer summary points such as the following:
- The Wise Men felt a call to which they could either respond or not. They went on a journey in response to their call.

- The Wise Men, like all of us, felt a spiritual longing. The decision to follow the star was related to that spiritual longing, a search for greater meaning. It was not an accident that they found God because they not only recognized their desire for God but also made difficult choices to leave their familiar worlds to go on a challenging trip to seek God.

5. Draw the students' attention back to the painting. Ask the students this question:
- When the Wise Men arrived, did their encounter with Mary, Joseph, and Jesus, as depicted here, give them any obvious reasons to offer respect and homage?

Share the following observations and questions and invite discussion:
- Notice that the Wise Men are wearing fancy clothes and crowns. Notice that Joseph has a plain gray robe and that the family is living with the animals in a stable.

- Does this child of these poor parents in these poor surroundings look like a king? What did these Wise Men recognize that kindled certain feelings in them and inspired them to get down on their knees in praise and worship?

Solicit answers.

6. Offer the following summary points:
- One might say that the Wise Men were spiritual "go-getters." They were in touch with their own desires for more in life, which enabled them to recognize the need to follow the star and to let go of their lives in order to conduct this search. We must be attentive to our own longings and give ourselves the opportunities to search for God when called.

- Something about Jesus was so compelling that they were able to adjust their own image of greatness to include his infancy and poverty. God can be surprising and has ways that are not the ways of humans. We need to be ready to find God's greatness in humble and other unexpected places.

- Sometimes a personal experience of the greatness of God is preceded by a longing or thirst for God and a journey like the one taken by the Wise Men. The experience of desiring more helps us recognize the fullness of God's grace when we are given such a special experience.

Mention that encounters with God call us to praise, reverence, and awe, and ask the following questions:
- Is it possible for people to know and experience such things today?

- Have you seen or heard of signs of such wondrous events?

Experiences of awe and wonder relate to God as creator of all that is awesome and wonderful. If the students don't mention any experiences that have inspired such awe in them, offer these suggestions: the communal experience of a World Youth Day, the generous heart of a saintly person, holding a newborn child, fearing that a loved one was hurt severely and then discovering that he or she was all right, or going on a pilgrimage or retreat. Remind the students that God calls to us in the ordinary and extraordinary events of life and that we must be prepared to recognize him and choose to respond.

Prayers of Thanksgiving

In this activity, the students will explore multiple reasons for offering prayers of thanksgiving.

Preparation

See pages 319-320 of the *CFH* for background information relevant to this activity.

Art

This activity uses *The Pilgrims of Emmaus,* on page 25 of *Beyond the Written Word.*

1. Before drawing the students' attention to the painting, invite them to close their eyes or to look at a neutral object. Lead them through the following imagination exercise:
- Recall a time when you sat down to a meal and someone said a prayer or blessing. Think about the details of the prayer and of the meal.

- Remember what the mood was at the table before and during the prayer.

- Remember how fast or how slow the prayer was recited.

- Notice whether the people not leading the prayer were paying attention.

- Remember whether the prayer changed anything about the mood at the table.

- If you can remember any of the prayer's words, think about what the prayer meant.

- Did the prayer influence the meal?

- Do you think that praying before a meal is worthwhile?

○ Return your attention to this room and this time, and open your eyes.

2. Invite the students to turn to *The Pilgrims of Emmaus,* and offer these instructions:
○ Compare this painting of prayer before a meal in *The Pilgrims of Emmaus* to the image of people at prayer before a meal that you just explored in your own memory. List on a sheet of paper the similarities and the differences between the scene in your memory and the scene in the painting. Focus on the mood, on the attention of the others gathered, and on the reason the prayer is being offered.

3. Ask the students to focus again on the painting. Ask them to consider whether they think the prayer moment in the painting, based on what they see, would have had an impact on the meal the three men were sharing. Ask them to note their answers on their sheets of paper and to include their reasons. Their reasons might include how closely the two people on the right are paying attention, the sense of reverence or the importance the painting conveys, the gentle, quiet mood portrayed, and the serious way God is being thanked for the meal.

4. Refer the students to their lists of similarities and differences. Invite them to reflect on needed changes to the scene from their memory for that prayer to have had a bigger impact on the participants' experience at the meal. Suggest to the students that they try one of the changes at the next meal they share with people.

Prayer in Times of Hardship

Students will recognize that private and shared prayer can invite God into experiences of suffering.

Preparation
See pages 319-320 of the *CFH* for background information relevant to this activity.

Art
This activity uses the following artworks from *Beyond the Written Word:*
- *Peter Walks on Water,* page 17
- *Christ on the Cross,* page 23
- *The Penitent Saint Peter,* page 28
- Detail from *Mystic Crucifixion,* page 24

1. Invite the students to examine the four paintings and to identify the one obvious detail they all have in common. (Something bad has happened and a form of lamentation is going on.)

2. Draw the students' attention to the disciples in the boat in *Peter Walks on Water* and to the women in front of the cross in *Christ on the Cross.* Ask them what the two groups have in common. (If the students do not have an answer, draw their attention to the hands and arms of the people in the paintings. They should be able to see that people in both paintings are reaching out to or touching one another.) Invite a discussion about why people do this when they face hard times together. Have the students recall times when they have witnessed this kind of reaction. How does God reach us in our sorrow through other people?

3. Next, draw the students' attention to Peter in *The Penitent Saint Peter* and to Mary Magdalene in *Mystic Crucifixion*. Ask them what the two figures have in common. (Peter is alone. Mary is talking to the angel but looks as though she is startled to learn she is not alone.) Even with all the people at the Crucifixion, Mary Magdalene was alone in her grief until she realized the angel had come in response to her prayers. Invite a discussion about why some people feel alone or prefer to be alone when they face tough times. How can God reach us in our suffering when we are alone?

4. Encourage a discussion that examines the apparent contradictions in dealing with hard times: reaching out to others for comfort and preferring to be or feeling alone. Expand the discussion to include how the communal and individual dimensions of loss, fear, grief, sadness, and anger have been integrated in the students' experiences. Have they seen people invite God into the suffering? Have they witnessed the grace of God when people have suffered with others and alone?

Activity Extension
Choose an event that was difficult for the school (for example, a death, accident, overdose, suicide) or the community (for example, the death of a soldier in a war zone, a natural disaster). Invite discussion on the communal and individual aspects of the lamenting that occurred following the event. How have the people who were affected reached out to God? Alone or with others? If the students name a recent incident, discuss how the class might pray together for strength and support.

Prayers of Petition
Students will explore several possible responses God might make to requests for help.

Preparation
See pages 318-319 of the *CFH* for background information relevant to this activity.

Art
This activity uses the following artworks from *Beyond the Written Word:*
- Detail from *Mystic Crucifixion*, page 24
- *The Penitent Saint Peter*, page 28
- *Gethsemane: "If it is possible, may this cup be taken from me."* page 21
- *The Descent of the Holy Ghost*, page 26

1. Remind the students that prayer often involves asking God for something. Mention any regular practice of petitionary prayer from class or from school Masses that would be familiar to the students. Ask them to name the kinds of requests usually made in such prayers.

2. Draw the students' attention to the paintings with the following reflections:

- Look at *Mystic Crucifixion.* Mary Magdalene is grasping the foot of the cross after Jesus has been killed. What request do you think she is making of God?

- Look at Peter in *The Penitent Saint Peter.* We know from the title of the painting that he is sorry for his sins. What do you think he is asking for? Might he be asking God for forgiveness or for the strength not to sin again?

- *The Descent of the Holy Ghost* shows the coming of the Holy Spirit to the disciples at Pentecost. Based on the faces and the postures or gestures, what do you think was the mood just before the Holy Spirit's coming? What is the mood at the beginning of the Holy Spirit's coming? What do you think the Apostles and Mary were praying for just before this moment arrived? Might they have been asking God for strength and support because they felt lost after Jesus's death?

- The painting *Gethsemane* shows Jesus praying in the garden at Gethsemane when he knew he was about to be arrested. We know what he was asking God for based on the title of the painting: "*If it is possible, may this cup be taken from me.*"

Summarize by noting that the prayer petitions discussed are the same petitions people place before God even today.

3. Offer the following questions and comments:
- How would God have seen each of these petitioners?

- Who is the model of prayer here?

- How does each person share something with us about prayer?

- Jesus, as Son of God, is the one who prays perfectly.

- Look at Jesus's face and note that although he is making a request, he knows his request might not be granted.

- What can we learn from Jesus at prayer?

4. Have the students form four or eight groups, depending on the class size, and assign one of the four paintings to each group. Tell each group to write a dialogue between God and the person or the people in the assigned painting, based on the following:
- In Jesus's case, the dialogue has to be with God the Father.
- In the case of Peter, the Apostles, and Mary Magdalene, the conversation could be with the Father, with Jesus, or with the Holy Spirit.
- Mary Magdalene's dialogue partner could be the angel, or messenger, from God as shown in the painting.

Give the groups the following instructions for writing their dialogues:
- You are writing a dialogue that shows how God would have responded or did respond to the petitions of persons in the paintings.

- The words of your dialogue have to be appropriate to the painting and to what you believe that God will and will not grant.

○ For those working with the Gethsemane painting: The words in the title are just the beginning; the rest of the words Jesus spoke are in the Bible, which has three versions. Use one of the versions, a combination of all of them, or your own adaptation of any or all of the versions. You can also give Jesus additional lines. [Direct the students to Matthew 26:39-44, Mark 14:35-41, and Luke 22:41-42 if they are unfamiliar with this story or want to compare the Gospel versions.]

5. Have the groups act out their dialogues. After each presentation, invite the rest of the class to say either that they agree or that they disagree that God would say what the dialog indicated. Invite the students to discuss how they might be prepared for a more in-depth dialogue with God the next time they make a request. Ask them what kinds of responses they might expect from God.

More About the Art

Art has the power to teach people, even if they know little or nothing of the artists or the circumstances. Nevertheless, additional information can help you use art with your students more effectively. This appendix contains a brief background for each artwork used in *Beyond the Written Word: Exploring Faith Through Christian Art*.

Creation of Adam, Michelangelo (Rome, Italy, 1512)

The nine panels in the ceiling of the Vatican's Sistine Chapel depict the first few chapters of Genesis. In the *Creation of Adam* panel, Michelangelo portrays Adam's waiting for God's vibrant energy to enliven him (the painting appears to combine Genesis 1:26-27 and Genesis 2:7-8). One common interpretation of this artwork is that the woman under God's arm is Eve, already alive in God's mind but not yet made human. Michelangelo was more a theologian than many other artists of his time, and he expressed his theology through art.

Adam and Eve, Komang Wahyu Sukayasa (Indonesia, 2001)

Komang Wahyu Sukayasa is from Bali, Indonesia. Because Bali is a "paradise" destination for tourists, the artist has painted a Balinese biblical paradise just before the Fall. The lush tropical vegetation, the birds, and the other animals reflect the richness of Bali in combination with elements from the artist's imagination—for example, giraffes are not native to Bali.

This painting *Adam and Eve* captures the abundance of God's Creation (see Genesis 2:8-9). It depicts Adam and Eve as they face the serpent. Eve is reaching for the fruit.

Bali's citizens are divided over whether to preserve the natural beauty of their land or to encourage more tourism through increased development. Does this painting portray the temptation to destroy paradise through development?

Wise Men from the East, Agha Behzad (Iran, 1958)

Agha Behzad chose to paint the visit of the Wise Men to the Christ Child—visitors who may have been men from the artist's own land centuries before (see Matthew 2:1-12). Behzad converted to Christianity and then used his skill as a painter to bring the Christian story to life for other believers in Iran, Persia, or "the East" in biblical times. Behzad's conversion came with a change in lifestyle—he overcame an addiction to both alcohol and drugs. Did he see himself as a man from the East who set gifts at the feet of and gave praise to the newborn King?

Detail of the *Moone Cross*, from a monastery (Ireland, ninth century)

The seventeen-foot *Moone Cross* was in pieces when it was found in the late nineteenth century and reconstructed. Legend indicates that it dates from the sixth century, a period widely considered to be the height of Celtic art. The *Moone Cross* was probably first erected at one of the monasteries that were common throughout Ireland. Though such stone crosses were possibly used as boundary markers, they also gave religious instruction. During this time period, the monks worked to preserve the Christian tradition. Depicting Bible stories in stone would have been a way to remind everyone, both the monks and the people who came to the monastery for services or as pilgrims, of the stories they had heard. Many people could not read at the time.

The base of the *Moone Cross* is carved with images from the Bible. The detail shown is a representation of the flight of the Holy Family into Egypt (see Matthew 2:13-15) and of the five loaves and the two fish (see Matthew 14:13-21, Mark 6:30-44, Luke 9:10-17, and John 6:1-15).

The Wedding at Cana, from the Jesus Mafa Collection (West Africa, late twentieth century)

In the late twentieth century, the leaders of Christian churches in West Africa decided they wanted a visual version of Bible stories for the people in their churches. They decided which stories were important to include in the collection and then hired an artist to paint them. The result is more than sixty scenes from Jesus's life told in the context of West African village life. Like any other portrayal of the wedding feast at Cana, the painting *The Wedding at Cana* from this collection contains the cultural trappings of the artist's own time or place because no one knows exactly what a wedding feast would have looked like in the first century.

Calming the Storm, Hanna Cheriyan Varghese (Malaysia, late twentieth century)

The work of Asian artists in a Christian arts magazine inspired Hanna Cheriyan Varghese to also focus her work on Christian subjects. She works in acrylics—*Calming the Storm* is an example—and batik.

By playing with the position of the sand-colored beach behind Jesus's outstretched arms and the light from the Holy Spirit, Varghese hints at the

Crucifixion in this painting. Perhaps she is suggesting that because Jesus died on the cross, all travelers in stormy seas, not just the Apostles, have his protection (see Matthew 8:23-27, Mark 4:35-41, and Luke 8:22-25).

The Multiplication of Loaves and Fishes, Michael Wolgemut (Germany, 1491)

Michael Wolgemut was an engraver, painter, and wood-carver in Germany in the late fifteenth and early sixteenth centuries. He taught the famous artist Albrecht Dürer. In *The Multiplication of Loaves and Fishes*, notice that the people are in German dress and that a typical Gothic castle or village is in the background.

In painting the miracle of the loaves and fishes (see Matthew 14:13-21, Mark 6:30-44, Luke 9:10-17, and John 6:1-15), Wolgemut condensed the whole story into one panel. While Jesus blesses and breaks the bread and the Apostles distribute the bread, the baskets of leftovers are already at Jesus's feet. Depicting several incidents in a painting was a common temporal distortion in religious paintings; the artist assumed the viewer knew the sequence of the story.

The Woman at the Well, Frank Wesley (India, late twentieth century)

Frank Wesley may be the best-known Christian artist in India. Wesley's Christianity is always in dialogue with the traditions of India, Hinduism, and Islam. You'll notice in this painting of the encounter between Jesus and the Samaritan woman (see John 4:4-42) that Jesus is wearing the saffron robes of an Indian holy man and is sitting in the half-lotus posture, a traditional yoga position. Yoga is a practical philosophical tradition that has some roots in Hinduism and Buddhism. Even today, in many rural parts of India, Jesus's speaking to a woman, especially one of another caste or ethnicity, would be considered strange.

Peter Walks on Water, Philipp Otto Runge (Germany, 1806)

Philipp Otto Runge painted in the Romantic style popular in the eighteenth and early nineteenth centuries. Romanticism, with its emphasis on emotion and subjective experience, was a reaction to the Enlightenment and the culture's emphasis on scientific reason.

Romantic painters often tried to induce an experience of the sublime, or the transcendent. Runge tried to express the oneness or harmony of the universe in his art. The storm, the sky, and the waves in this painting *Peter Walks on Water* are as much a reflection of God's transcendent power as is Peter's faith that enables him to walk on water (see Matthew 14:22-33).

The Good Samaritan, Rudolfo Arellano (Nicaragua, 1981–82)

In the 1960s on the islands of Solentiname in Nicaragua, Fr. Ernesto Cardenal established a spiritual community that developed into an arts community where poor farmers, or *campesinos,* learned crafts to help improve their economic situation. Rudolfo Arellano is one of the better-known artists to emerge from the Solentiname community. He paints in what is known as a primitive style.

The setting for the parable of the good Samaritan (see Luke 10:30-37) is the rocky desert road to Jericho. A Nicaraguan *campesino* would not know the terrain of Judea, so when he heard the parable he would envision a road familiar to him—a road like that painted by Arellano in *The Good Samaritan.* Likewise, he would interpret the passing holy people as the holy people he knew: priests, nuns, and bishops.

The Good Samaritan (After Delacroix), Vincent van Gogh (France, 1890)

The Dutch painter Vincent van Gogh began to study art at age twenty-seven and eventually moved to Paris where he was influenced by French artists. His painting of *The Good Samaritan* uses the same basic outline as the identically titled painting by Eugène Delacroix, an early nineteenth-century painter, but makes vivid changes to the color and the texture of the painting.

This painting of the parable of the good Samaritan (see Luke 10:30-37) was made shortly before Van Gogh's suicide. In declining mental health (probably a form of epilepsy), he had spent some time in an asylum, where this painting was probably made. Notice the bandage that covers the top of the left ear on the injured man's head. Van Gogh had cut off the lower part of his own left ear just a year earlier. Delacroix shows the scene in reverse, with the injured man's right side showing and the bandage slightly above the man's ear.

The Last Supper, Sadao Watanabe (Japan, 1984)

Sadao Watanabe sought to integrate Christian faith with the traditions of Japan. He created artworks with traditional Christian content but used traditional Japanese techniques. *The Last Supper* is done in the traditional Japanese art of stencil dying. As in batiking, the artist begins with an idea of the finished product, but because the process is not exact, the final artwork may not emerge as intended. The element of chance in the creative process requires the artist to trust the nature of the fabric and the dyes.

The Last Supper focuses on the moment when Jesus is breaking the bread to share, and in this painting, Judas is hiding the bag of silver behind his back (see Matthew 26:17-30, Mark 14:12-25, Luke 22:7-38, and 1 Corinthians 11:23-26). The Apostles are sitting on their knees on the floor in traditional Japanese fashion.

Gethsemane: "If it is possible, may this cup be taken from me." Ni Ketut Ayu Sri Wardani (Indonesia, 2002)

Ni Ketut Ayu Sri Wardani is a young woman from Bali, Indonesia, who has painted some powerful, vivid explorations of Christ's Crucifixion, of his agony in the garden at Gethsemane, and of Mary's suffering. Sri Wardani is especially moved by the suffering Christ endured for us. Many of her paintings have Scripture quotations in the titles.

Sri Wardani uses strong brush strokes and colors like lashings to wake up the viewers of her paintings to the power and significance of the reality of Christ's actions. In *Gethsemane*, the artist depicts Jesus's hands in such a way that they seem to quiver. Artists have long been interested in what Jesus Christ endured during his time in the garden (see Matthew 26:36-56). Sri Wardani seems to have focused on his human emotions.

Christ Crowned with a Crown of Thorns, Albrecht Altdorfer (Austria, 1518)

Albrecht Altdorfer was a German painter known for his skillful use of landscape and architecture in biblical and historical scenes. He tended to paint emotional scenes using the landscape, the architecture, and the color to contribute to the emotional effect. This painting is one of a series of altar panels in an abbey church near Linz, Austria.

The clean white of Jesus's tunic contrasts with the exotic architecture of the setting and the luxurious colors of the soldiers' clothes. Only the drops of blood falling from Jesus's face, where the thorns have broken the skin, disturb that pure white. In an interesting use of artistic license, Altdorfer puts Jesus in the white cloak. Matthew says Jesus wore a red cloak and Mark has him in purple (see Matthew 27:27-31 and Mark 15:16-20). What might Altdorfer have been trying to highlight by putting Jesus in white?

Christ on the Cross, Giovanni Domenico Tiepolo (Venice, Italy, mid-eighteenth century)

Giandomenico Tiepolo, as Giovanni Domenico was known, came from a family of artists and learned his craft from his talented father. He preferred to paint scenes from contemporary life, but he did a fair number of religious paintings. In this time period, the Church was not the main patron of the arts, and many secular patrons did not want religious art.

The positioning of the crosses in *Christ on the Cross* allows the relationship between the mother and the son to be central to the composition. The light on Jesus's tortured body emphasizes the suffering Mary has witnessed. The blue cocoon in which Tiepolo wraps Mary seems to give her strength to witness the ongoing horror. Tiepolo combines elements from the four Gospel accounts of the Crucifixion (see Matthew 27:45-56, Mark 15:25-41, Luke 23:39-49, and John 19:28-30).

Detail from *Mystic Crucifixion*, Sandro Botticelli (Florence, Italy, mid-1490s)

Sandro Botticelli was a Florentine contemporary of Leonardo da Vinci. A favorite of the Medici court in Florence, Botticelli was one of the artists commissioned by the Pope to paint the walls of the Sistine Chapel.

While working for the Medici family, Botticelli was part of an intellectual circle that was trying to integrate Christian views with those of the classical world of ancient Rome and Greece. Later, Botticelli was influenced by the preaching of reformers and developed a new sense of religious devotion.

Mystic Crucifixion was painted during that later time. Though the synoptic Gospels place the women at some distance from the Crucifixion scene (see Matthew 27:45-56, Mark 15:25-41, and Luke 23:39-49), Botticelli accepts John's account and places Mary Magdalene near the cross (see John 19:17-30).

The Pilgrims of Emmaus, Henry Ossawa Tanner (United States, 1905)

Henry Ossawa Tanner was an African American artist from Pennsylvania. He began his art studies with Thomas Eakins, an American Realist painter, in Philadelphia. After some years of struggling to make a living as an artist in the United States, Tanner emigrated to Paris. In Paris he achieved enormous success and respect, though he always considered himself an American.

Henry Ossawa Tanner was always concerned with matters of faith and, especially later in life, focused primarily on biblical themes in his paintings. When Tanner returned to the Emmaus story (see Luke 24:13-35) some years after *The Pilgrims of Emmaus* was made, he painted the next moment in the story—when Jesus vanishes from the sight of the two disciples.

The Descent of the Holy Ghost, Sandro Botticelli (Italy, late fifteenth century)

Sandro Botticelli may be best known today for his painting *The Birth of Venus*. In that painting, Venus stands naked in a scallop shell that floats on the sea, with her unruly red-blond hair blowing around her and an attendant ready to wrap her in a robe. But his paintings of the Madonna are what have always stirred people. *The Descent of the Holy Ghost* is a rare depiction of an older Mary.

The painting portrays the coming of the Holy Spirit at Pentecost (see Acts 2:1-8). Even though Mary has been through the horror of her son's torture and death and his amazing return to be with his friends for a few weeks, her face reveals the same willingness to surrender to God's will that she demonstrated during the Annunciation and in speaking the Magnificat.

The Holy Spirit, from Saint Peter's Church (Fallbrook, California, late twentieth century)

Stained glass has been a significant religious art form since the tenth century. Many traditional European religious images appeared in the stained glass in the new churches built during the late nineteenth and early twentieth centuries in the United States, but increasing experimentation with contemporary religious symbolism in stained glass began appearing during the latter half of the twentieth century. This window, *The Holy Spirit,* combines some of the old with the new.

The Holy Spirit has long been depicted with a variety of symbols, including the dove, rays of light, and tongues of fire. In this window, these ancient symbols are shown descending to the big blue marble that is planet Earth, which is visible from space. In the flow of one lead line that begins and ends above and below the Holy Spirit's left wing, the artist has depicted an invisible layer of protection, or grace, surrounding the planet.

The Penitent Saint Peter, Simone Cantarini (Italy, 1640s)

The art style of seventeenth-century Europe is called Baroque, a style marked by realism and an emphasis on emotions and spirituality. The penitent Peter was a popular theme. Cantarini painted Peter in extreme close-up so that viewers could experience an intimate connection with him.

All four Gospel writers describe Saint Peter's denial of Christ after his arrest (see Matthew 26:69-75, Mark 14:12-25, Luke 22:54-62, and John 18:15-18, 25-27). Peter's lifelong penitence was important in seventeenth-century spirituality, and people were encouraged to cry over their sins if they woke during the night as Peter was said to have done every night. The intensity of Saint Peter's emotions is depicted in the painting, and he appears to be close to the viewer. This device was intended to bring sinners closer to saints. Peter was especially important, not only because he was a lifelong penitent, but because he was an example of how easy it is to fall into sin, even when one loves Jesus as deeply as Peter did. Paintings such as *The Penitent Saint Peter* would remind viewers to be vigilant against falling into sin themselves.

The Ladder of Ascent, from the Monastery of Saint Catherine at Mount Sinai (Egypt, twelfth century)

The Ladder of Ascent is an icon that was painted or *written* (the official term for the creation of an icon) by an anonymous monk in the twelfth century, about six hundred years after the monastery was built. One of the early abbots of the monastery, circa AD 600, wrote a treatise called *The Ladder of Divine Ascent*, describing the attainment of virtues as akin to the steps on a ladder. He later became known as John Climacus, or John of the Ladder.

In his dream at Bethel (see Genesis 28:10-12), Jacob saw angels going up and down a ladder to heaven. By the early 600s, John Climacus knew that the way to heaven was a function of actively living a life for God. Those who entered monasteries tried to make a life of prayer and virtue easier by removing themselves from the temptations of the world, but temptations, or demons, are everywhere. The imagery is applicable in and out of the monastery.

The Last Judgment, Italo-Byzantine painting (thirteenth century)

In the world of Orthodox Christianity, the traditional Byzantine way of painting icons in a flat, two-dimensional manner continues today for legitimate theological reasons. At the beginning of the Italian Renaissance, artists began experimenting with a shift from the symbolic nature of the two dimensions to the representational nature of three. This painting retains the composition of an icon of the Last Judgment but begins to experiment with adding a realistic third dimension. The fabric on the angels is still flat, but Jesus's garments and the faces of Jesus and the angels have a shaded three-dimensional quality to them.

The image of the Last Judgment comes from Matthew 25:31–46. The painting *The Last Judgment* has symbolic elements: the groups of people at Jesus's right and left hands; the actions, wings, and garments of the angels; and the *mandorla,* which is the almond-shaped blue glory around Jesus's whole body. Combined with the symbols are representational elements, such as the faces of Jesus and the angels. Viewers are supposed to see the representational elements as being just as real as they, the viewers, are. The artwork accomplishes this feat through shading and other tricks used to show depth, an approach that would have been offensive to an Eastern icon writer.

Italy served as a kind of border between the Eastern Church and the Western, or Roman, Church. The city of Ravenna has the westernmost of the early Eastern churches, a seventh-century church full of icons in the two-dimensional style. The Roman Church had never had the same issues about art that spawned iconoclasm (icon-breaking) movements in the Byzantine church, so the theology behind the style had not mattered in the West. Italian artists were free to paint the Last Judgment any way they wanted.

Additional Resources

This appendix has background material to help deepen your knowledge of art. It also has information on the resources recommended throughout th e teaching guide.

The Church and Art

The Relationship Between the Church and Art

Teachers with some sense of art but little knowledge of the relationship between the Church and art have a smorgasbord of literature available to them. I recommend these two books:

De Borchgrave, Helen. *A Journey into Christian Art.* Minneapolis: Fortress Press, 2000.

Drury, John. *Painting the Word: Christian Pictures and Their Meanings.* New Haven, CT: Yale University Press; London: National Gallery Publications, 1999.

Both books have theological analyses of selected works of Christian art.

The History of Christian Art

Those who are comfortable with using art in religious education but are interested in knowing more of the history are invited to try these resources:

Baggley, John. *Doors of Perception: Icons and their Spiritual Significance.* Crestwood, NY: St. Vladimir's Seminary Press, 1995.

Eco, Umberto. *Art and Beauty in the Middle Ages.* Translated by Hugh Bredin. New Haven, CT: Yale University Press, 1986.

Jensen, Robin Margaret. *Understanding Early Christian Art.* London; New York: Routledge, 2000.

Theology and Art

For those interested in the theology that convinced the Church to allow the making and viewing of images when many wanted to forbid images completely, I recommend the following books, although Schönborn's may be the easiest for the contemporary reader:

John of Damascus, Saint. *On the Divine Images: Three Apologies Against Those Who Attack the Divine Images*. Translated by David Anderson. Crestwood, NY: St. Vladimir's Seminary Press, 1980.

Schönborn, Christoph. *God's Human Face: The Christ-Icon*. Translated by Loathr Krauth. San Francisco: Ignatius Press, 1994.

Theodore the Studite, Saint. *On the Holy Icons*. Translated by Catherine P. Roth. Crestwood, NY: St. Vladimir's Seminary Press, 1981.

Explorations of theological aesthetics are available from Frank Burch Brown, whose *Religious Aesthetics* addresses matters of taste and moral correctness as well as other topics; Alejandro R. García-Rivera; and Fr. Richard Viladesau, whose *Theology and the Arts* is digestible by the average reader.

Brown, Frank Burch. *Religious Aesthetics: A Theological Study of Making and Meaning*. Princeton, NJ: Princeton University Press, 1993.

García-Rivera, Alejandro R. *A Wounded Innocence: Sketches for a Theology of Art*. A Michael Glazier Book. Collegeville, MN: Liturgical Press, 2003.

Viladesau, Richard. *Theology and the Arts: Encountering God through Music, Art, and Rhetoric*. New York: Paulist Press, 2000.

Reference Materials

Sources of Additional Art

The Internet search engine Google, as well as other search engines, offers the option of searching for images. The variety of images available is vast. Countless other sources are on the Internet for those willing to search for them. When finding art this way, check the Web site to see whether permission to use the art must be requested for educational use.

Most public libraries have a collection of art books, and some bookstores that sell publishers' overstock have art books at discount prices. Museums sell slides and books of artworks from their own collections.

Do not overlook local sources of Christian art. Schools and churches have windows, the stations of the cross, baptismal fonts, and other decoration that you can explore with your students.

Visual Literacy

I suggest the following basic books to learn about the language of art:

Cavallaro, Dani. *Art for Beginners*. New York: Writers and Readers Publishing, 2000.

Dondis, Donis A. *A Primer of Visual Literacy*. Cambridge, MA: MIT Press, 1973.

Ask a colleague who teaches art to recommend a basic art history book you can use as a general reference.

Dictionary of Christian Symbolism

This dictionary of Christian symbolism or iconography is worth checking out: Apostolos-Cappadona, Diane. *Dictionary of Christian Art*. New York: Continuum Publishing, 1994.

Art Concordance

Textweek's art concordance is without equal in any search for art related to biblical themes. Go to *www.textweek.com* and find the link to the art concordance.

Further Reading

Further Reading

Frank Meshberger's theory about Michelangelo's *The Creation of Adam* can be further explored at *www.bbc.co.uk/dna/h2g2/A681680*, accessed December 13, 2004.

Bali's conflict over development is discussed by Jakarta-based writer Keith Loveard in "The Paradise Paradox" at *www.baliguide.com/paradise_lost/ index.html*, accessed September 16, 2004.

Artist Agha Behzad's conversion is recounted by his friend William McElwee Miller at *www.persianwo.org/behzad-miller%20christmas%20card.htm*, accessed September 16, 2004.

More information about the Jesus Mafa Collection can be found at *www.jesusmafa.com/anglais/histof.htm*, accessed September 16, 2004.

Profiles of artists Hanna Cheriyan Varghese and Ni Ketut Ayu Sri Wardani can be found at *www.asianchristianart.org*, accessed September 16, 2004.

More information about the artist Sadao Watanabe can be found at *www.elca.org/artwork/sadao_watanabe.html*, accessed September 16, 2004.

Artist Henry Ossawa Tanner is profiled at *www.pbs.org/wnet/ihas/icon/ tanner.html*, accessed September 16, 2004.

Pope John Paul II tells the story of the monks of the Monastery of Saint Catherine at Mount Sinai in a February 26, 2000, homily, which can be found at *www.cin.org/jp2/jp000226.html*, accessed September 16, 2004.

Acknowledgments

The scriptural quotations contained herein are from the New Revised Standard Version of the Bible, Catholic Edition. Copyright © 1993 and 1989 by the Division of Christian Education of the National Council of the Churches of Christ in the United States of America. All rights reserved.

With the exception of the "Becoming the Religious Artist" activity, all the material in chapter 1 and on handout 1-A is adapted from "Seeing and Being Seen: A Visual Approach to Religious Education," PhD dissertation, Boston College, 2001, by Eileen Mary Daily.

The excerpts from the Nicene Creed on pages 26, 28, 29, 34, and 36 are from *Catholic Household Blessings and Prayers.* Copyright © 1988 United States Conference of Catholic Bishops, Inc., Washington, DC, pages 374-375. All rights reserved.

To view copyright terms and conditions for Internet materials cited in this book, log on to the home pages for the referenced Web sites.

During this book's preparation, all citations, facts, figures, names, addresses, telephone numbers, Internet URLs, and other pieces of information cited within were verified for accuracy. The authors and Saint Mary's Press staff have made every attempt to reference current and valid sources, but we cannot guarantee the content of any source, and we are not responsible for any changes that may have occurred since our verification. If you find an error in, or have a question or concern about, any of the information or sources listed within, please contact Saint Mary's Press.